CORNISH WAR & PEACE

The Road to Victory
- and Beyond

Second edition, revised, 1998

Front cover
Commemoration of the 50th Anniversary of D-Day at Tolverne, May 1994
(Peter Newman)

Back cover
Top: The ceremony at Landeda, Brittany, in 1994, held to commemorate both the Christmas Escape (1943) and the Liberation (1944)
(Derek Carter)
Bottom: Helston, 8 May 1945, when VE and Flora Days coincided
(Susanne Carter)

Commemoration of the 50th Anniversary of D-Day at Trebah *(Derek Carter)*

Viv Acton & Derek Carter

CORNISH WAR & PEACE

The Road to Victory
- and Beyond

Landfall Publications

First published 1995 by
LANDFALL PUBLICATIONS
Landfall, Penpol, Devoran, Truro, Cornwall TR3 6NW
Telephone 01872-862581

Copyright © Viv Acton Derek Carter 1995

A CIP catalogue record for this book is available from the British Library.

ISBN 1 873443 21 8

All rights reserved. No part of this book may be reproduced or transmitted in any form or by any means including recording or photocopying, without permission in writing from the publisher.

Printed by the Troutbeck Press
and bound by R. Booth Ltd, Antron Hill, Mabe, Penryn, Cornwall

Queen Elizabeth inspecting Wrens in Falmouth.
Pat Wingate front right. (Chapter 4) (RCPS)

CONTENTS

ACKNOWLEDGEMENTS		6
INTRODUCTION		7
CHAPTER 1	Tolverne	9
CHAPTER 2	"Down at the Ferry Boat Inn"	18
CHAPTER 3	Men Who Dared Death	27
	The Christmas Rescue	39
CHAPTER 4	Women at War	49
CHAPTER 5	Lines around the World	59
CHAPTER 6	Radar - the Secret Weapon	66
CHAPTER 7	"The Eyes and Ears of All Our Defences"	80
CHAPTER 8	Cornish Airfields	87
CHAPTER 9	Victory and Peace, 1945	104
	Victory in Europe	104
	A Bitter Hand to Hand Campaign	114
CHAPTER 10	Leonard Cheshire	122
CHAPTER 11	Wild Goose, Swallow and Nerve Gas	128
CHAPTER 12	"Now Win the Peace"	135
	Problems of Peace	135
	Optimism for the Future	142
POSTSCRIPT	The Festival of Britain	153
APPENDIX	1. The Tragedy of the *Lancastria*	156
	2. Special Construction	156
	3. American Forces & D-Day	157
	4. The Return of the *Mutin*	159
	5. The Secret Army	159
	6. The Lavatory before the Flush	160
BIBLIOGRAPHY		161
INDEX		162
OTHER BOOKS FROM LANDFALL		167

ACKNOWLEDGEMENTS

We are indebted to many people who have shared their memories and willingly given us help. These include:

Joyce Aldous, Leonard Andrew, Freddie Bell-Scott, Judy Birkin, Lloyd Bott, Peter Boving, Norah Butler, Susanne Carter, I J Collett, Jean-François Derrien, Margaret Diplock, Joan Donkin, Nigel Eva, Peter Gilson of the Royal Cornwall Polytechnic Society, Mary Godwin Librarian for Cable & Wireless, Sally Henderson of St Teresa's, Leigh Hooker, Tony Inwards, Marjory Jones, Dick Laming, Bill Lester, Daniel Lomenech, Imogen Longbottom, Barbara Lorentzen, Judy McSwiney, Elizabeth & Peter Newman, Penpol & Point WI, Harold Pickles, Michael Pollard, Peggy Porterfield, Ernest Putley of the Defence Research Agency, Jean-Claude Renault, Sir Brooks Richards, Maud Rickard, Peggy Riley, St. Day Historical & Conservation Society, Stuart Smith, Arthur Thomas, Dunstan Thomas, Richard Thomas, Ann Thompson of Helston WI, Harold Thompson, Richard Townsend, Gerry Trevain, Staff of Truro Reference Library, John Tucker, Bill Turner, Pamela West, Victor Williams, Patricia Wingate, Bruce Wood.

INTRODUCTION

Cornish War and Peace is a sequel to *Operation Cornwall 1940-1944* in two ways. First of all it gives more details on some of the topics discussed in the earlier book as well as dealing with several aspects of the war in Cornwall scarcely mentioned before. Secondly it goes on to the end of the war, to the victory celebrations and the immediate aftermath.

It seems clear that the Second World War, either directly or indirectly, brought great changes to Cornwall. Cornish people found themselves in parts of the world they would never normally have expected to see, and strangers arrived in Cornwall who would scarcely have heard of it before. The Duchy suddenly assumed strategic importance, which is still shown today by the largest naval helicopter base in the country, as well as by a variety of communication systems on cliffs, downs and beaches.

Communications and community spirit are two of the themes of this book. Writing it has left us with the impression that the increasing speed of communications since the war has helped to undermine the close-knit society that existed during and before it.

Viv Acton
Derek Carter
March 1995

NOTE
The use of the symbol * in the text indicates that this topic has been dealt with more fully in *Operation Cornwall 1940-1944*.

1. TOLVERNE

One morning in late May 1994 a pleasure boat chugged towards the narrow waters of King Harry Reach for its destination, Smugglers Cottage at Tolverne. When it passed the low promontory of Turnaware Point American voices buzzed with comment as the visitors gazed at the now-quiet, wooded slopes. On the other side of the river Trelissick House, with its green fields sloping down to the water, appeared and then disappeared from view as the boat moved into the deep passage between the steeply-wooded banks and passed beneath the towering hulls of redundant merchant ships.

Anticipation mounted with the boat rounding the bend and sailing into the wider waters beyond the ferry crossing. There on the east side just above the water and almost camouflaged against the thick woods, stood the thatched cottage. But it was not the beauty of the scene that caused the cries of amazement and the lumps in the throat, but the old military vehicles lining the beach with the Stars and Stripes proudly waving above.

D-Day commemoration board at Tolverne. (P. Newman)

Tolverne

These were no ordinary American tourists being taken on a Fal River trip, but veterans of the Landing Ship Tanks who fifty years previously had left the shores of Britain for the beaches of Normandy. Here at Tolverne during the first few days of June 1944, guns and lorries rumbled down the road and soldiers marched on to the long jetty thrusting out into the water where the boats were moored. Thirteen LSTs left from Polgerran, Hard 5, as this embarkation beach was then called, for the bloody beach of Omaha, and on board the pleasure boat were some of those veterans who had survived the Normandy invasion and were now returning to commemorate the past.

The part played by Tolverne in the huge armada of Operation Neptune was the climax to four years of participation in the war. It was in the summer of 1940 that Cornwall first suffered from the direct effects of hostility. After the evacuation of Dunkirk more troops were sent secretly across the Channel, many embarking from Falmouth, but before long Paris fell and France surrendered. Refugees poured across the Channel into Falmouth and other Cornish ports on every boat that they could find, and this stream was continued as the Channel Islands were taken over at the end of June.

With French airfields now under German control Cornwall was within reach of their bombers as Falmouth soon discovered. During the early days of July the town and docks suffered from fatal raids and the River Fal winding past Tolverne was used by the German pilots as a guide before turning down river to attack. Invasion of the country seemed imminent and preparations were hurriedly stepped up to face this menace.

A constant watch was kept on the coast for enemy activity and as further protection, the Fal River Patrol, a water version of the Home Guard, was formed by Captain Bennett Webb in August to guard the upper reaches of the Fal from Truro to Turnaware Point. Smugglers Cottage at Tolverne was ideally placed for this patrol and for about two years they used one room as a guard room, where the men could spend the night time in between their watches on the water. Rodney Newman, whose home this was, also hired out two of his boats to them, the *Mystery* and the *Lizard*, to make up the complement of five that was later increased to seven.

These patrol boats, armed with light machine guns, had to negotiate the creeks and their mudbanks every night without using any lamps. One crew member who enjoyed his pipe was ordered to invert the bowl so that the glow of the tobacco would not be seen. If there were any air raids while they were on shore at Tolverne, their only protection was the overhanging trees clinging to the steep banks of the river.

Tolverne

Smugglers Cottage before the embarkation hard and new road were made, with Mystery, Rodney Newman's boat used by the Fal River Patrol. (P. Newman)

Tolverne

A telephone book, carefully preserved by Rodney's son Peter Newman, logs the calls they made in the course of their duties, the first entry being 30 September 1940. The telephone wires were buzzing with activity in the early hours of the morning of 14 April 1941, when German planes roared up the river. Eleven calls were made that night and the Police War Diary records the incident as happening at 04.45 in woodland at Tolverne, where four high explosive bombs were dropped on "2 old French destroyers moored in Tolverne Reach. *La Suippe* sunk immediately and the *Couquerante* is in sinking condition. Only a watchman was on board - 'slight wounds'". In fact there were two watchmen and Peter Newman believes that the wounded men were brought to the cottage to have their injuries attended to by his mother and that these boats were being used by the Free French.

In a BBC broadcast some years later, Mr New, a member of the patrol, described what it had been like to be awoken "in the dark on a cold dripping morning" when they would stumble down to the landing stage. "After hauling on the ice-cold mooring lines, entangled with seaweed, and jerking an equally cold and reluctant motor engine into life, we'd set off downstream straining our eyes for familiar river marks, and avoiding if we could invasion craft of all shapes and sizes." They would then exchange reports and news with the Falmouth Naval Patrol Boat. By this time the guard room had been moved to Lime Quay, at the junction of the Fal and Truro Rivers, because of preparations that were beginning for the opening of the Second Front.

The tragedy of Pearl Harbor in December 1941 had brought America into the fighting. Before long, convoys were crossing the Atlantic bringing troops and equipment into Britain and their high command was wanting to take the war directly into Europe. Although this was thought premature and North Africa became the main war zone at first, plans began to be put into operation for the time when the Second Front would be feasible. If German-occupied Europe was to be invaded a huge number of boats would be needed loaded with men, vehicles and stores. If all this was confined to existing ports there would be bottlenecks and easy targets for German bombers, so the search was on to find beaches which could be used and Tolverne and Turnaware were both chosen on the Upper Fal.

At both Tolverne and Turnaware access roads had to be built and beaches made hard enough to take the weight of heavy vehicles. The Admiralty took over Smugglers Cottage as a headquarters for the building at both places and Rodney Newman was kept busy ferrying men and equipment between the sites. For a year there was constant coming and going as the beaches were prepared. At Tolverne hundreds of tons of granite were brought by lorries and boats to build up a wide, flat area by

Tolverne

the water. Flexible "matting" made up of concrete pads reinforced with steel wire was then laid down, and the jetty was constructed stretching out into the river. (See Appendix 2.)

Meanwhile the new road to Tolverne required the blasting away of rock to reduce the gradient as it approached the shore. When the concrete that was laid by the beach had dried out it was almost white in colour so the surface had to be covered by a thin layer of tarmac to darken it and so stop unwelcome German attention. Protection was needed for the site especially as the river acted as a guide to German pilots, so 40mm AA guns were set up on either side of the water.

By the summer of 1943 the Americans were beginning to come into Cornwall, first of all the sailors, the Construction Battalion or Sea Bees as they were known, and then the soldiers, mostly from the 29th Infantry Division. So many were pouring in by the early months of 1944 that the county was described as "almost the 49th State of the Union".*

The new roads built down to the hards were found to be too narrow for easy movement of large vehicles and so they were widened by the Americans with hard concrete; the join between the two sections and the differences in texture are still noticeable today on the approach to Tolverne. Strict security was kept on these sites with notices and armed guards to warn off the over-inquisitive.

Life for the Newman family must have been very difficult especially when their cottage was used as living accommodation for some of the senior American officers. The room that is now the bar became a military office with thirteen telephone lines installed. The Newman children were sent away to live with relations but Rodney and his wife Mabel were allowed to stay in the rooms at the back. Rodney and his boats were needed for transport which could be done more secretly by water than by road and there must have been constant comings and goings between Tolverne and the Falmouth Hotel, the main American headquarters in the area. Wherever Rodney and Mabel went they were accompanied by armed guards; secrecy was vital. Mabel could not even go shopping without her escorts.

Rodney had another job to do, which was deception. German planes would fly over for reconnaissance and to photograph any new activities, but the American presence in the county had to be kept as secret as possible. Camps, tanks guns and other vehicles were heavily camouflaged or hidden in woods, as at Tolverne and Turnaware, but boats were not so easy to hide. The Fal, with its steeply-wooded banks by the narrow but deep water of King Harry Reach, was ideal and as D-Day approached more and more boats were being built. To confuse the enemy dummy boats were also built out of wood and sacking, some being constructed in

Tolverne

Lamouth Creek almost opposite Tolverne. Rodney Newman had the job of towing these boats, sometimes down the river in Carrick Roads, sometimes up-river, just to create confusion not only for German airmen but also for any spies that might be around, and this area was reputed to have had more than its fair share.

Most of the young American men based here had never seen active service. What was worse, many of the soldiers had never seen the sea or experienced boats until they crossed the Atlantic to come to Britain. Yet these same men were expected to take part in a sea-borne invasion, climbing in and out of boats weighed down by heavy equipment and under enemy fire. Much of their time in the South-West was therefore spent in training.* The most famous training grounds were in Devon, on Dartmoor, at Saunton Sands in the north of the county and the most notorious, Slapton Sands on the south coast where tragedy struck during exercises a few weeks before D-Day.

Slapton was not the only area to have its tragedy. On a smaller scale training near Tolverne also ended disastrously for some, and Peter Newman can remember his mother talking about the bodies that were brought to the cottage and laid out in a nearby shed.

Some time during these hectic weeks the Supreme Allied Commander, General Dwight Eisenhower, was believed to have made a visit to his men here. Unlike today when a visit of this importance would be splashed across every newspaper, movements of military men were kept secret and no one officially knew of this visit. However Rodney and Mabel were introduced to him when he landed at Tolverne.

The climax to all this training and weeks of waiting came in early June 1944. Restrictions on civilian movement had become much tighter since the beginning of April. In mid-May soldiers were moved to their embarkation camps, the "sausages" extending alongside the main roads leading to the loading areas. There they were given their final, detailed briefings. The Fal was bursting with craft being prepared for the crossing of the Channel. Then, the day after Falmouth received its last and perhaps worst air raid, the whole ponderous operation began to swing into action. The roads became increasingly filled with vehicles all moving inexorably in one direction, the embarkation points. Roads were closed to all but military traffic and the areas near the embarkation beaches were completely banned to civilians.

Loading at Tolverne began at midnight on 1 June, using the hours of short summer darkness to avoid unwelcome scrutiny. Two LSTs (Landing Ship Tanks) loaded at a time and for the next few hours the guns and vehicles rolled slowly aboard from the hard into the open bows of the vessel while the men, no doubt very apprehensive of their future, walked

Tolverne

along the jetty to embark. When full the boats moved off to make way for the next two.

LSTs were the largest of the landing craft, 328 feet long, 50 feet wide and with a crew of over one hundred men. More than a thousand of these vessels were built in the States, many being used in the Mediterranean for the North African and Italian campaigns before sailing to Britain to begin preparations for D-Day. One of these was LST 5, which dropped anchor in Falmouth on 9 May 1944 by the Messack Buoy. Over the following days the crew were allowed no shore leave, but were kept busy with toxic gas drills, gun drills with simulated air attacks and firing practice at targets drawn behind aircraft.

Then on 1 June the large vessel moved slowly up-river to Tolverne to begin loading with LST 393 at 03.00. Twelve hours later the vessel was full with seventy-two vehicles of the 635th US Army Tank Destroyers and over two hundred officers and men. They moved down-river to stand by in Falmouth Harbour and then on 4 June they became part of convoy B-3, which moved off at ten in the morning, only to return again to harbour for another day, because of the stormy weather.

On board was seventeen-year-old Gunner's Mate Bill Lester from New York State. He had enlisted about six months previously and

LST 5, which loaded at Tolverne for D-Day, on Omaha Beach. (B. Lester)

Tolverne

was now knowledgeable in the operating of the 20mm and 40mm anti-aircraft guns on board, new ones having been recently installed at Penarth in South Wales. "Our convoy was huge; the LST count alone was thirty four. We arrived off Omaha Beach in the afternoon of 6 June. It was impossible for us to go in and unload as the beach was in chaos, so we stood by off the beach to receive the wounded in a make-shift surgery on board." (See Appendix 3.)

The fighting for this beach was the most desperate of all the five invasion beaches and casualties were high, but determination, courage and vital help from the heavy guns of battleships eventually won the day and the foothold on Europe was gained.

LST 5 remained off Omaha until 8 June, off-loading the vehicles into Rhino Ferries, and then it left with its cargo of prisoners of war, and the wounded, both Americans and Germans. Over the following weeks it returned to both this beach and Utah, and was caught in a storm that raged up the Channel. The *Yank Army Weekly* of 6 August 1944 reported:

> "So intense was the gale that the ship (LST 5) was unable to maintain position and was dragging her anchors along the coast. Nevertheless, because of her bulk she was far better off than most craft in the vicinity.
>
> "As the storm progressed, the smaller vessels ran out of supplies - food, water, fuel. They came alongside and signalled for help. An LCI was short of water, another was low on fuel. A subchaser was running out of food. ..... And No. 5, with her capacious fuel and water tanks and large storage space, was able to help everyone."

Cornwall felt strangely quiet in the following days, although not all the Americans had left. At Trelissick, the base for the 776th Anti-Aircraft Weapons Battalion, the men, such as Leigh Hooker (See Chapter 9), were still deployed on the gun-sites around the Fal and Helford in case of German retaliation, but by mid-July they also had left for Normandy.

Meanwhile the vessels were doing a commuter run between Falmouth and Normandy, ferrying out men and supplies and bringing back the wounded. The Falmouth Harbour Master's Journal, recording all the non-naval shipping movements, shows tremendous activity in June and July especially with American merchant ships such as the *SS JC Bearnie* which arrived on Saturday 10 June to load at Tolverne. LST 5 returned twice more to Falmouth, and as Bill Lester writes: "Between D-Day and late October, we made at least thirty round trips across the Channel. Our biggest fears were E boats and mines. Our sister ship, LST 6, was sunk by a mine. At least eight LSTs were lost in the Channel."

16

Tolverne

In November this vessel was handed over to the Royal Navy in Belfast, and was then taken out to Malaya, where the war against Japan was still raging. For Bill and his ship-mates there was another spell in the South-West, to embark from Salcombe for the return home across the Atlantic. It was hoped that the war would be over by Christmas, but this was not to be and months of hard campaigning were still ahead before Victory in Europe could be celebrated the following May.

No wonder that many memories were revived during the summer of 1994 when commemorations and reunions were held in Normandy and elsewhere. Plaques at Trebah on the Helford, and Turnaware and Tolverne on the Fal, now mark the places where these men embarked, to remind us of the horrors and deprivations of war as well as the bravery of so many individuals.

Bill Lester writes: "My return to the UK and France was very emotional at times. The high points were seeing the area around Smugglers Cottage at Tolverne and the services at the invasion beaches. Lord only knows how many men my ship alone disembarked on those beaches who did not make it back."

Smugglers Cottage seems an unlikely place to have witnessed all these momentous events, surrounded as it is by woods and water and welcoming the holiday visitor with barbecues and cream teas, but even before the boards and plaques for the 1994 commemorations were erected, the observant visitor might have noticed the concrete pads that now form the garden walls, which once took the weight of military vehicles and guns as the men embarked from Polgerran Hard 5.

D-Day commemoration plaque at Trebah. (D. Carter)

2. "DOWN AT THE FERRY BOAT INN"

The rich, the famous and the bomb-weary came to Helford Passage to stay at the newly-built Ferry Boat Inn during the war. An inn had stood on this site for generations, marking the ferry crossing over the river to the village of Helford, but in the mid-thirties the new owners, Commander Douton and his wife Kathleen, pulled down the old inn and had the new one built "planned rather like a ship, being a long, low white building which snuggles into the cliff," as Norah Butler (née Reynolds) remembers from the early war years when she worked here. A warm welcome, good food, comfortable beds in cabin-like rooms and plenty of hot water from an enormous boiler and "the largest taps I have ever seen fitted to the baths," were an attraction to "mandarins" from the War Office and the Home Office, as well as a variety of people from London, Bristol and other badly-bombed cities, delighted to enjoy some peace and quiet. One pilot who spent many of his leaves here was the night-fighter pilot, John "Cat's Eyes" Cunningham (Chapter 6), who came here with his mother and friends.

Stars from stage and radio stayed here including "the absolutely stunning Leslie Mitchell", later one of the first TV announcers, and Michael Powell, the film director. The latter arrived just after the finish of his film *The 49th Parallel*. "He spent a lot of time in the office concocting press releases and establishing the viewing rights of the film worldwide."

Even before the war the inn had been popular. "A lot of the visitors were Lords and Ladies," recalls Maud Rickard, who worked there as a parlour maid and waitress. "No walking down Passage Hill for them. They used to arrive in their own cars driven right to the door." One of the pre-war visitors had been Von Ribbentrop, who was then the German Ambassador in Britain. He was a guest at Glendurgan and arrived at the inn with his hosts for dinner one evening. He kissed the ladies' hands, spoke beautiful English, was generous to the staff and "most people thought he was charming," recalls Norah Butler, but Kathleen Douton did not like him at all. "She thought evil emanated from him and said that he would become one of Hitler's henchmen with Germany bent on war."

Maud remembers the coming of the war: "They blacked out the hotel on the Friday before war was declared on the Sunday. It was so awful. Everywhere was dark, no lights anywhere. There had always been lights around and now there was nothing."

"Down at the Ferry Boat Inn"

The old Ferry Boat Inn about 1930. (N. Butler)

Page from the brochure of the Ferry Boat Inn about 1939. (N. Butler)

There are bathrooms in plenty—8 of them—to serve the 10 double rooms and 9 single ones.

Even the passages are heated in cold weather, though Helford Passage enjoys a most temperate climate, being the mildest spot in England, sheltered from all cold winds.

"Down at the Ferry Boat Inn"

Norah arrived the following summer to help with the running of the inn. She could not have come at a worse moment, because it was June 1940, the time when Allied troops had been driven back through Belgium and France by the remorseless German forces and were being evacuated from Dunkirk and later from the Cherbourg Peninsula. Civilians were also fleeing and she found Falmouth in ferment. "It was full of confused refugees everywhere you looked. These poor people, having left their countries, not knowing what was going to happen to them or how they were going to live, having left everything behind. It was all very tragic. This was the first time that I had seen Falmouth Harbour and it was so crowded with ships of all shapes and sizes that you couldn't put a pin between them."*

The holidaymakers at the Ferry Boat soon found their quiet, peaceful time shattered by the "well-heeled refugees" who crowded in there and the situation became chaotic. "Baron Rothschild was there with members of his family, as were also the eminent French scientist Mademoiselle Curie, some hysterical members of the Comédie Française, and the worried wife of the former French ambassador to Germany, with her little boy, not knowing what had happened to her husband." A host of other French and Belgian people flowed through the inn. Beds were put in the drawing room, the dining room was crowded out at every meal time, taxis came and went and the telephone never stopped ringing.

The new Ferry Boat Inn about 1939. (N. Butler)

"Down at the Ferry Boat Inn"

This was the start of a real fear of invasion; the Ferry Boat Inn, right beside the waters of the Helford River, could soon be ringing with the sound of German boots, or the skies above could be filled with enemy paratroopers. Each coastal area had to make its own contingency plans to evacuate people. A meeting was held at the inn for the civilian organisations, the Coastguards, the Red Cross, the LDV (Local Defence Volunteers, later the Home Guard) and the ARP (Air Raid Precautions). The inn would be the collecting point for the local people, from where they would be led by secret paths to secure houses inland. One of the wine cellars was to be emptied and become an air-raid shelter and a special 2lb bag of granulated sugar, marked "For Invasion Purposes Only", was allocated to the inn. This was not for emergency food rations, but for tipping into the petrol pump which had fuel for the ferry, "in the teeth of the German landing party." (Just enough fuel was supplied to run the ferry for a week a month, otherwise the boat had to be rowed.)

The sugar never needed to be used for this purpose, but there was an Invasion Alert one night some time later. A telephone message came through from naval headquarters in Falmouth that a strange boat had been seen coming towards the Helford river. Norah, who was in temporary charge at the inn, sent the ferryman, Ronnie *(pictured right)*, to alert the Home Guard and Commander Warington Smyth, the local Naval Officer who lived up-river at Calamansack where there was no telephone. A motor cycle anti-parachute patrol arrived, making enough commotion to wake up the guests. Local people began assembling ready for evacuation and Norah wondered if it was time for the sugar to be used. Some people were becoming frightened and upset so they made tea and "actually began having a lot of fun." They heard later that it was a false alarm, caused by a local patrol boat which failed to answer a morse signal from the Falmouth Guard Ship. The whole defence system had been put on alert from Plymouth westwards.

"Down at the Ferry Boat Inn"

There were other scares. One day a plane was seen swooping low over the river. There was a huge splash and a bomb fell straight into the water. A few days later there was a whistling noise. "We rushed outside and saw a bomb dropping from the skies. We all stood there open-mouthed. Then it landed on the other side of the river where it made a huge crater in a meadow." (This was where Helford Car Park is today.) One night two sea mines exploded on the outskirts of Mawnan Smith.* "The noise was absolutely tremendous." On another occasion a magnetic mine was discovered floating near the inn, just fifty yards away. "It was bobbing about in a pool at the bottom of the cliffs, and a platoon of soldiers were sent to watch over it until it could be defused."

Norah had a particularly worrying experience when she was rowing over the river in the ferry boat with the housekeeper's three grandchildren. "We were all laughing as we rowed across and then suddenly a plane came out of the clouds, swooped down on us and shot us up before zooming off down the river. It made me absolutely furious."

The labour shortage meant that the staff had to work very hard. Maud recalls, "We used to start work at 7am and go on until everything was cleared away in the evening. Then we all met at the staff table and had a cup of tea together before departing for the night." When the hotel was closed in the winter all the blankets and curtains had to be washed. She was joined at one time by a girl from Redruth. "She was a proper card and was well aware of workers' rights. Before too long we had two hours off every day and an extra 2s 6d a week. At that time I was receiving 10s a week, which all went home, but I kept the tips. The Commander saved up my weekly 2s 6d and tips and gave it to me at Christmas, so that I could buy new dresses. This amounted to fifteen pounds. I had never been so well off in all my life. They were a lovely pair to work for. They really looked after us."

For most of the time guests at the inn would have found Helford Passage and the river a quiet place where they could temporarily forget the fears and dangers of war. However, some of the guests were probably aware that this peaceful retreat hid activities that were far more warlike. Admirals, Air Marshals and Generals stayed here and Maud remembers one particular visit. "We didn't know who was coming, but we all knew it was someone important. We were peering out of the windows, guessing who it might be, when a great army truck arrived. Out of it popped this little man." It was General Montgomery. "He stayed with us for three days shortly before he went to the Middle East," recalls Norah. "He neither drank nor smoked or even conversed much. He was a puzzling but a fascinating man. All he seemed interested in was the army and tactics and doing what he could to help win the war." "All he had in his bedroom,"

"Down at the Ferry Boat Inn"

says Maud, "was his Bible and his Prayer Book. You wouldn't have known he was there otherwise."

What drew men like this to the Ferry Boat Inn? Did they come just for a short break in routine or were there other reasons? Norah recalls that Ridifarne, one of the large houses further along Bar Road, was taken over by Commander Gerald Holdsworth and his "cartography unit". Sometimes Norah went there to have tea with his wife, Mary, who had been an artist, and she showed her pictures that she had done and also maps. But something did not ring true in all this. They had several boats, including a French crabber, but they always seemed to go sailing at night. Why should map makers want to do their work in the dark?

A clue to this mystery was one of the first visitors that Commander Holdsworth booked in to the inn, soon after his arrival at Ridifarne. This was Captain Slocum who, Norah discovered much later on, was the operational head of Naval Intelligence. Ridifarne was the local headquarters of the SOE (Special Operations Executive) formed to "set Europe alight," according to Winston Churchill. From here agents and equipment were taken secretly to secluded Breton coves and from there other agents, as well as Allied airmen who had been shot down, were brought back to Britain.

"The crews spent quite a lot of time in our bar" recalls Norah. "By a freak of the licensing laws the Shipwrights Inn on the other side of the river in Helford, had to close at 9.30, but we could stay open until 10.00. It was not unknown for some of them at the Shipwrights to ring for the ferry and Ronnie would row over and pick them up for a final drink at Passage. They were usually quite merry, but they never let anything slip. They were really very good the way the secret was kept."*

Some local men were involved with these activities including Maud's future husband, Deacon Rickard. In the early days of the war, before he had joined the Royal Navy, he used to row across from his home on the other side to see her every evening, having a special permit to do this from Lieutenant Sharp, who commanded the patrol boat in the Helford and lived with his wife at the inn. After he joined up he was in Falmouth and then moved up the river on to the *Mutin*, one of the SOE's French boats. But in November 1942, soon after the Allied landings in North Africa, most of the SOE with Commander Holdsworth and Lieutenant Brooks Richards, his second-in-command, moved out to the Mediterranean to carry on their undercover work there and Deacon went with them.

Maud remembers a story of Deacon's when he was in Algiers. "A boat came alongside the *Mutin* with an Arab in it. Deacon said to Commander Holdsworth, 'What on earth are we up to now picking up these Wogs?' Apparently the man was filthy dirty and stinking to high

"*Down at the Ferry Boat Inn*"

The *Mutin* today. Once used for secret wartime activities; now used by the French Navy as a training ship. *(D. Carter)*

"Down at the Ferry Boat Inn"

heaven. A little later, after a shower and a shave, he appeared as the smart Lieutenant Brooks Richards. He had of course just returned from an intelligence operation behind the lines." (See Appendix 4.)

In the summer of 1943 a beautiful three-masted yacht, *Sunbeam II*, was towed into the river and moored nearly opposite the Ferry Boat Inn. This was to become the headquarters of another Intelligence organisation, the SIS (Secret Intelligence Service), which had been operating from Falmouth with an advanced base on the Isles of Scilly. The two groups were rivals, but they were now each under the command of Commander Warington Smyth's two sons: Bevil commanded the SOE and Nigel the SIS, so possible tensions between them were eased. It was from the Helford that a surf boat was towed out to meet MGB 318, to rescue airmen and agents from the western end of Brittany on Christmas Day 1943. Tests on surf boats had been made at Praa Sands, when the surf was running high, to evaluate their stability, and now the men from the Helford units were to put their skills to good effect. (Chapter 3.)

Most of this activity was carried out unknown to the local people or to most of the visitors who stayed at the inn. Business was brisk in the summer. The weekly charge for full board was about five to seven guineas, the same level as before the war. "The Doutons thoroughly disapproved of war profiteers, particularly as so many of our guests were service people,"

Norah Butler with a guest at St Anthony-in-Meneage 1942. Note the defensive wall in the background. (N. Butler)

"Down at the Ferry Boat Inn"

recalls Norah. "The bar in the summer did a roaring trade and we were often quite busy in the winter as well."

Norah eventually left to join the Wrens, and the inn was then sold to a company. But its popularity continued and she says "David Niven, the film star, vowed that it was his favourite pub, and came to stay regularly after the war. I also remember a happy post-war song-writer who wrote a hit song, 'Down at the Ferry Boat Inn,' whilst he was staying there." She concludes, "The bar is much the same as in my day there and I still visualise Jimmy Lewarne and Ernie Rickard and all the locals chatting as they sat by the fire nursing their half pints and talking to the mysterious 'cartography unit'."

The bar of the Ferry Boat from 1939 brochure. (N. Butler)

TARIFF

This Inn is Fully Licensed

'Phone : MAWNAN SMITH 78

DAILY (Three days or under)

March, April, May & June	16/-	each person
July	18/6	,, ,,
August and September ...	21/-	,, ,,
October ...	16/-	,, ,,
Nov., Dec., Jan. and Feb.	13/-	,, ,,

WEEKLY

March	4½ guineas each	
April, May and June	5	,, ,,
July	6	,, ,,
August and September ...	6½	,, ,,
October ...	5	,, ,,
Nov., Dec., Jan. and Feb.	4	,, ,,

Bed and Breakfast, **10/-** Winter . . **12/6** Summer.

Terms for Easter, Whitsuntide and Christmas holidays on application.

The only extra is early morning tea.

MEALS

Breakfast	3/-
Lunch (Hot)	3/-
,, (Cold)	2/6
Cornish Tea	1/6
Dinner	5/-

Garage Charges

1/- per day for each car.

Dogs

1/- per day each Small Dog.
2/- ,, ,, ,, Large Dog.

PROPRIETOR :

Commander A. R. C. DOUTON, R.D., R.N.R. (Retired),
The Ferry Boat Inn, Helford Passage, nr. Falmouth, Cornwall

3. MEN WHO DARED DEATH

On a summer afternoon in June 1942 a French fishing fleet was scattered off the south-west coast of Brittany trawling in a light swell near the Iles de Glenan. Armed convoys passed heading north, and patrolling Heinkels criss-crossed the sky above. In spite of this evidence of war all seemed peaceful. As the afternoon slowly gave way to evening a line of five German corvettes steamed purposefully past, just as a small white sail could be seen approaching one of the distant fishing vessels, at first slowly tacking to and fro, and then as the corvettes disappeared, moving steadily towards it.

After it had made fast on the seaward side of the trawler, a strange procession of people emerged on deck and, as the small boat rose on successive waves, they clambered on to the other boat helped aboard by willing hands - a woman, three young children and then two men encumbered with luggage and a babe-in-arms. They disappeared quickly below as petrol, oil, tobacco and food were hurriedly passed down to the sailing boat. The transaction was completed in five minutes. The small boat cast off, turning in a wide circle back towards the land while the trawler moved off seawards just as a Heinkel appeared in the distance on its usual patrol.

This was no innocent Breton trawler but one crewed by men of the Royal Navy who had crossed the Channel from Cornwall and were now to return there after a successfully-completed mission. The second-in-command was a young Frenchman, Daniel Lomenech, and now also on board was the French agent "Rémy" with his family escaping from the clutches of the Gestapo.

Daniel Lomenech had also been an agent for a time until his situation had become too dangerous. While still only a teenager living with his parents at Pont Aven in south-west Brittany, he had shown great courage and determination in escaping to Britain after the German occupation. This was easier said than done with the Channel to cross. First he had persuaded friends in the tunny fishing industry to take him out with them into the Bay of Biscay where he hoped to find a British warship. After fifteen days and no sight of the Royal Navy he was forced to return home.

He then found some fishermen on the north coast willing to take him to England but only in return for money. This he raised by selling cigarettes and other stores previously hidden by retreating units of the

Men who Dared Death

Daniel Lomenech. *(R. Townsend)*

British army, who had told him not to let them fall into German hands. Armed now with the necessary cash he returned to the north coast and this time was successful in persuading the men to set sail. He eventually was able to transfer to a Cornish trawler in the Channel, in spite of the French crew, who had used his money to buy drink and were thoroughly drunk by this time.

Once in England he hoped to join the Royal Navy but, after careful vetting by British officials, he agreed to work for the intelligence services where there was no age limit because he was still too young for the forces.

Men who Dared Death

Information on the German defences of the Channel coast was urgently needed, and he twice returned secretly to France.

On both occasions his journeys back to Britain with information came close to disaster. For the first one he made his plans with the same fishermen who had helped him previously. This time they went to pick him up from the wrong place and to while away the time went ashore for a drink, leaving the boat badly moored. It drifted off to be rescued by Germans who found evidence on board of visits to Britain, so making it impossible for the boat to be reclaimed. With a crew but no boat Daniel in desperation got money from his father, bought a crabber in Cameret and made a very hasty retreat.

On the second occasion a trawler was to pick him up from the Iles de Glenan and then transfer him to a submarine, HMS *Sea Lion*. This worked successfully except that a second man was also involved whom Daniel did not trust. He overcame the problem with the help of friends, who got the man so drunk that they were able to bundle him senseless into the boat, for the short journey to the islands. However, Daniel was now compromised and could no longer act as an agent, but his knowledge of the Breton coast and fishing vessels was too great to lose.

Over the next few months he made four Channel crossings by submarine as Conducting Officer to make contact with a French fishing boat from Guilvinec belonging to friends of his. Using submarines in this way was not ideal as the opportunities for rendezvousing with French agents was too limited. (The navy needed the boats for regular patrols.) So a new method was tried out following discussions with Daniel.

This was to make use of a French trawler that could cross the Channel and then mingle undetected amongst the fleet. A search began for a suitable vessel, many having been brought over by refugees from France, and finally with the help of Daniel a 60-foot, diesel-powered boat was chosen. This was *Le Dinan*, which had been used on patrols out of Newhaven and was now known as *N51*. After an engine overhaul and other necessary work had been completed she eventually was moved from Shoreham westwards to Dartmouth in February 1942 and later to Cornwall. A British crew was used, men from the patrol service who in peacetime had been North Sea fishermen and so were used to the cramped conditions and the smell of fish that still pervaded her.

Daniel by now was old enough to join the Royal Navy and was made First Lieutenant on the *N51*, but by the time the boat was nearly ready its use was in doubt, as the group of agents in Lorient had broken up. Before long, however, another French agent took over this part of the organisation. This was Guilbert Renault-Roulier, alias "Rémy", alias "Raymond".

Men who Dared Death

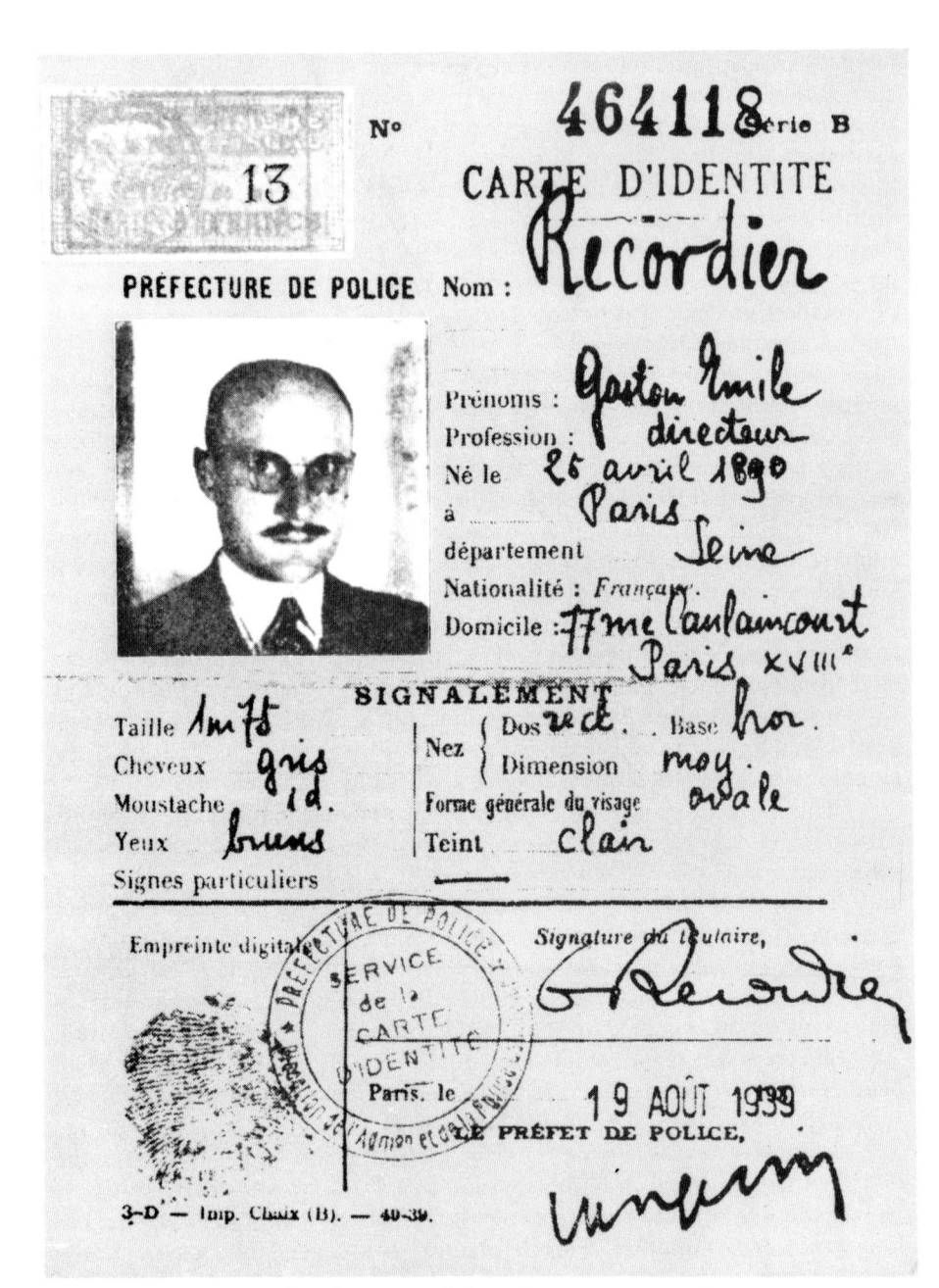

False identity card for "Rémy". *(J-C. Renault)*

Men who Dared Death

Like Daniel, Guilbert had escaped to Britain after the fall of France, but unlike Daniel he had the responsibility of a wife and a growing family still in France. He returned to organise intelligence networks along the whole of the coast from Brittany to the Spanish border and became one of the most important of the French agents as head of "Confrèrie Notre Dame". In the same month that *N51* went to Dartmouth a successful raid was made on the German radar station at Bruneval, about 12 miles from Le Havre. Information vital for the success of this raid had come from his organisation.

Radar was very much the secret weapon during the Second World War used by both the British and the Germans and both sides tried to reduce the effectiveness of each other's systems. (Chapter 6) For a year a watch was kept on the German battleships *Scharnhorst*, *Gneisenau* and *Prinz Eugen* in port at Brest to try to prevent them from breaking out and adding to the havoc of disasters at sea. However in February 1942 they did just that, helped by the subtle jamming of British radar, by increasing the intensity slowly so that it would not be noticed.

So the successful raid on Bruneval later in the month, carried out by a combined air and amphibious operation, raised morale as important radar equipment was captured there and brought back to Britain for further study. A month later a second successful raid was made on the French coast, this time on St Nazaire to destroy the huge dry dock, the only one on the Atlantic coast large enough to accommodate the *Tirpitz*. This expedition set out from Falmouth, returning there in greatly depleted numbers a few days later.*

Guilbert was also in London about this time when future rendezvous arrangements were being discussed and when he mentioned the growing danger for his family with the possible need for their evacuation. Although *N51* was nearly ready for use it was all very secret and her effectiveness had still to be tested, so she was not mentioned at that time to Guilbert, who returned to France a few days later by air. But within a few months the whole of his family was to be thankful for this vessel and its crew.

During April and May *N51* made two voyages across the Channel using an advance base off Tresco in the Isles of Scilly. Here in this remote place the necessary changes could be made to re-paint her from the usual naval grey to the appropriate French fishing boat colours; and of course the distance to Brittany was reduced. On the first occasion in April they were due to make contact with "Rémy", but just before they sailed they heard that he was not ready, so they made this a trial run, gaining the satisfaction of finding many similar French boats on the fishing grounds and provoking no interest from passing German convoys. They planted a "post box" on an island off Concarneau and took photos of the French coast.

Men who Dared Death

However there were problems with the captain who was constantly drinking. Daniel, hearing a row in the crew's quarters, went to investigate and found him standing there with a grenade in each hand ordering the men to surrender to the Germans. Daniel calmed him down by promising to take them into a Breton port, then led him to the hold where he locked him in with a bottle. He took over command and began to sail back to Cornwall when an explosion rocked the boat. In the hold they found the captain dead, having primed a grenade. When asked many years later if he was ever afraid on these dangerous operations, Daniel replied, "Never. Never. I was too young."

N 51, when the "post box" was planted. (R. Townsend)

The new commander on the second voyage was Steven Mackenzie, an officer in the intelligence services. "Rémy" was ready this time, but in spite of waiting for two days at the rendezvous point they made no contact with him. From a distance they witnessed a British raid on Lorient not knowing that mines laid during the attack prevented any vessel from leaving the shore, so they were foiled here by their own side and left rather

Men who Dared Death

disconsolate, feeling that the new system for rendezvous would be regarded as a failure.

However the events of the following month made up for their disappointment because not only were they able to make contact with "Rémy" but they also rescued the whole of his family. His eldest daughter Catherine, then aged 12, has told the story of this rescue: "In June 1942 we were in a very difficult position. The Boches had our description and their police were searching everywhere for us. Some friends of ours had been arrested and tortured; in fact everything was going very badly." They went into hiding, Catherine, her mother Edith, her younger sister Cécile, and her two brothers, Jean-Claude and baby Michael, or Mic-Mic, as the family called him.

Very early on the morning of Wednesday 17 June they were taken by horse and cart to the little port of Pont Aven, Daniel Lomenech's home, where Rémy's contact boat, *Les deux Anges*, was berthed. They hid below deck, "Rémy" with baby Mic-Mic and another agent, "Leger", in the tiny forward hold, and the other four in the two baggage departments, or as Catherine describes them, "sort of boxes which stank of fish and were cluttered up with socks, pants, trousers, shoes and berets."

They got through the Customs check undetected, but for thirteen hours they had to stay there, sea-sick and cramped, and "nearly gave up the ghost", but luckily for Catherine and Jean-Claude they found some welcome oblivion in sleep and were unaware of their father's fears about the possible failure of the rendezvous. Then about four o'clock in the afternoon, Alex, one of the three-man crew, said, "I can see a boat from Cameret which is not supposed to be on this bank. It must be their trawler."

They waited for two hours for the fixed rendezvous time of six o'clock with the crew watching the trawler closely. "Yes, yes it is them," said Alex. "Those fellows there are pretending to trawl, but that does not deceive an old hand like Alex."

Just before six the corvettes appeared, seemingly steering straight for them, but to their relief passed by, as did a patrolling Heinkel. Only then could the transactions take place and wife, children, luggage and mailbags be quickly bundled aboard. "When we arrived on board, the welcome was very moving, the sailors were wonderful," wrote Catherine. "They offered us jam and other rich things which we did not feel like eating. We had to keep asking for the bucket."

They had to remain below deck for another day and a half, but then "Papa, who was disguised as a sailor, told us that we could go on deck because we were in English waters and that we had the English flag flying."

33

Men who Dared Death

Changements de physionomie du colonel Rémy

Portrait du
colonel Rémy

Portrait avec
lunettes et avant
pousse de la moustache

The changing faces of "Rémy." Compare with the photo on page 30. (J-C Renault)

"Rémy" had just witnessed the arrival of two Beaufighters sent out from Cornwall to protect them from possible U-boat attacks. The planes swept over them, separated and turned in wide circles low over the sea. "Rémy" wrote, "They reminded me of seagulls which fly tirelessly until they see their prey."

The children emerged on deck with cries of joy but looking pale, with the exception of Mic-Mic who was fresh and rosy-cheeked. The crew brought them warm coats, for the early morning felt chill, and at long last they were able to enjoy the sandwiches and hot tea prepared by the cook.

The excitement was marred as the Beaufighters were leaving on the arrival of two Hudsons to take over escort duties. In Catherine's words "One fighter, which was trying to do an acrobatic manoeuvre, hit the water with its tail and, unable to straighten up, crashed into the sea. A search was immediately carried out but nothing could be found except the undercarriage which was floating on the surface." The fruitless search for survivors delayed their arrival in the Scillies, but they eventually reached New Grimsby, Tresco, at three in the afternoon.

Yet another incident happened here to make even more memorable an already unforgettable day. This was the arrival of the MGB, the

Men who Dared Death

gunboat, to take the passengers on to the mainland. It might have been regarded by the crew as just another stint of duty, but "Rémy" was highly respected and the navy made the most of the occasion.

The sun was shining and all was quiet and peaceful when the drone of the engines was heard in the distance and then, in the words of Steven Mackenzie, "Round the headland appeared the MGB, pendants fluttering green and white, bow wave creaming in the deep blue water and from her loudhailer came the martial crash of a Sousa march, the music resounding from the hills." Fifty-two years later Jean-Claude recalled this sight with some emotion and believed that the Marseillaise was played in their honour. Catherine wrote, "The crew were standing to attention on deck and the officers were saluting us. On the mast was what looked like a necklace, made up of all the flags of the Allies."

"Rémy" missed this spectacle, because the clear, green waters had enticed him to dive in for a swim. Hearing the music and his children's cries he had clambered back on deck to witness the end of this "truly royal reception. I felt that I was completely out of place in swimming trunks and dripping with water and I hid myself."

They were quickly encouraged on board and were off again, with scarcely time to say goodbye to the men who had rescued them, "MacKenzie, Lomenech, Townsend, the delightful crew." "Rémy" carefully carried with him plans of the coastal defences of France, which had been passed on to him by a painter and decorator who had smuggled them out of the German headquarters in a roll of wallpaper.

N51 had already been joined by another French trawler, P11, and in due course more were added to form what became known as the Inshore Patrol Flotilla, the base of which was moved from Dartmouth to Falmouth in 1942. By September 1942 it had become obvious that a regular monthly voyage would be needed to take supplies and bring back mail from the "Raymond" organisation, (the new code-name for Guilbert, alias "Rémy") because once he had seen his family safely installed in Britain, he had gone back to France.

Some months later, when Guilbert used the same escape route again, the naval officers noticed the great care with which he handled a large bundle. No doubt believing that this was some secret piece of equipment he had smuggled out, they were amazed to see him unwrap a flowering azalea bush, a present for Madame de Gaulle.

During the following winter N51 needed new engines, and another trawler, A04, under the command of Richard Townsend, continued to keep the line open in spite of bad weather. In due course a specially designed boat was built to look like P11 but with very powerful engines and by the early summer of 1943 it was ready to take over from the slower trawlers at

Men who Dared Death

a time when the hours of darkness were fewer and when speed could be vital.

In June 1943 the whole organisation was moved to the greater seclusion of the Helford River, where the SOE (Secret Operations Executive) had been based since late 1940.* On the banks of the Helford just east of Helford Passage, the isolated houses of Ridifarne and Pedn Billy had been used as headquarters for the SOE, the "mysterious cartography unit." (Chapter 2) Now their sister group was given the luxurious accommodation of a privately-owned three-masted schooner, *Sunbeam II*, which was moored off Helford village, or as Leigh Hooker, an American soldier stationed there in 1944 remembers, "She sat mid-river right opposite my gun." (Chapter 9) These two organisations were headed by brothers, Nigel and Bevil Warington Smyth, which helped to reduce the suspicion and rivalry that had existed between the two groups.

During the autumn of 1943 a series of arrests in France brought to an end the "Raymond" line, but work still continued from the Helford base partly because the growing numbers of Allied bombing raids over Germany and occupied Europe increased the number of pilots who needed to be rescued when planes had crashed, and the events leading up to the Christmas Day rescue are a story in themselves. (See the following section.)

The contrast between the comparative peace and quiet on this river and the tension of the operations to Brittany - the danger from the elements; the fear of discovery and capture; the possible failure to make contact knowing that this might be a matter of life or death to the agents, their helpers and families - must have been very great. Leisure time and social life, however limited, were no doubt a vital antidote to stress.

Imogen Longbottom, who was a Wren on the staff at Pedn Billy, remembers the happy evenings dancing in Mawnan Smith village hall with one of the officers from the *Sunbeam*. "No disc jockey or taped music in those days but a proper band, that seemed to play non-stop for hours on end." There was a visit with him for tea with Lady Seaton at Bosahan. "We left the boat tied at the foot of steps which led up through semi-tropical vegetation to the house, and in the garden there was the biggest and most beautiful magnolia tree in full flower."

There was a night-time fishing expedition up the river with the men of the *Roger Juliette*, one of the French vessels used by the SOE, where a net was laid in a half-circle from the shore. "After much pulling and tugging the shore turned silver with the catch". The *Sunbeam* sometimes held ENSA concerts on board to give some variety to the limited entertainment available, but visits to the local pubs were the most usual way to deal with stress and these could sometimes get a little out of hand.

Men who Dared Death

Gilbert Renault-Roulier, "Rémy", receiving the Commandeur de la Légion d'Honneur from Lord Louis Mountbatten at Broadlands, Hampshire. *(J-C. Renault)*

Men who Dared Death

Gerry Trevain, a visiting RAF wireless technician based at St Eval, who had short stints of duty in Helford to install communication systems in the boats, remembers one such visit spent in a grand sing-song around the piano, which no one wanted to stop at closing time. The men therefore carried the piano out of the pub and loaded it on to their moored dinghy nearby. They then rowed across to their ship, the *Mutin*, and tried to manhandle it on board; not the easiest of operations in the dark on a moving boat. The piano slipped and ended up in the river. When these organisations were disbanding in 1945 Imogen recalls that when the *Sunbeam* left her anchorage, the joke that went round was that the sound of breaking gin bottles could be heard for miles.

There was another group of men and boats that became increasingly involved in the secret voyages across the Channel and these were the men of the "little ships", especially the Motor Gunboats of the 15th Flotilla. The French fishing boats were useful but slow and the RAF tender used by the SOE from the Helford, although fast, was vulnerable in bad weather. The gunboats had originally been built to protect coastal convoys and for air-sea rescue work, but as they were relatively inconspicuous with powerful engines capable of a maximum speed of 26 knots and with a cruising range of five hundred miles they were very useful for crossing the dangerous open waters of the Channel.

MGB 329 *(V. Williams)*

Men who Dared Death

The SOE had used Motor Gun Boat 314 from Dartmouth in late 1941 and early 1942 for landing and embarking agents and it was this boat, with her captain Duncan Curtis, that led the brave armada of "little ships" with the floating bomb of HMS *Campbeltown*, up the River Loire to the massive lock gates at St Nazaire in March 1942.*

In this same month Motor Gun Boat 318 was sent from her base at Yarmouth to Dartmouth to be the first boat in the 15th Flotilla, soon joined by others. Later, in early 1944, even more powerful boats were built, the new type 500, with a top speed of 31 knots, a cruising range of two thousand miles, and with a draught shallow enough for the rocky Breton coast. From Dartmouth secret operations were continued across to France, but for any operation in the west of Brittany, Falmouth was used as the port of departure from the base at Coastlines Wharf.

The gunboats, the secret operations both in Falmouth and on the Helford and perhaps most of all the French men and women ready to risk death, were all concerned in the episode of the Christmas rescue.

THE CHRISTMAS RESCUE

The build up for this rescue began several weeks earlier and showed how disastrous poor communications and bad weather could be for these secret operations. On 9 September an Allied bombing raid on the Renault works near Paris resulted in the shooting down of the American bomber nicknamed "Wee Bonnie". All the men survived but the pilot and five of the crew became prisoners-of-war. The other five managed to avoid capture and became evaders, the name given by the Americans to those trying to escape. One of these was the co-pilot Harold Thompson.

He landed in an apple tree in a northern suburb of Paris and, after quickly getting rid of his parachute and flying gear, he hid himself in a large garden with a small vineyard. Before long a frail-looking old lady slowly approached, snipping off dead vine leaves as she came. She pushed a note into his hand which read, "Welcome to France. You are safe where you are. We will have instructions for you later. Don't leave your place." He was soon taken to a safe house where for nearly three months he found himself cared for, entertained, protected and eventually helped to escape by one of the underground organisations, which risked everything to aid airmen like him who had been forced to bail out over occupied territory.

For seven weeks he remained in this area, looked after mainly by André, a veteran of the First World War and "absolutely fearless". The navigator of the bomber, Henry Rowland, "Rollie", was also with him and André would bring them breakfast in bed. Then they would spend the day

Men who Dared Death

reading English novels provided for them or going out visiting André's friends and relations. They went canoeing on the Seine, had bike rides in the countryside, and shortly before they were passed further along the escape route, André took them sight-seeing to Paris. All this took place under the noses of the German authorities.

André and his associates organised identity cards for them and then took them to catch the crowded train to Cherbourg. There was a nasty moment or two when the gendarmes checking papers kept Rollie back, but he put up a good show as a deaf mute, which was their cover to overcome the language barrier, and he was allowed through. It was only when they were close to their destination that they realised that all the people in their part of the train were either guides or other American evaders.

At Cherbourg they changed trains for Landernau in Brittany where, with sleeping German officers nearby, the four guides now with them made out work permits and passes for them. The two men in charge of this expedition were Pierre Hentic, who used the pseudonym "Mao", and Pierre Jeanson, alias "Sarol". When they arrived they found the station swarming with German soldiers, but at the check-point the chief gendarme let them all through. Over one thousand German soldiers were stationed near the coast in this area, at the villages of Lannilis, Landeda and Plouguerneau; the very area that the Résistance organisation used for their escape routes.

Harold and Rollie spent some hours hidden in a wood shed, but not before the lady of the house had regaled them with hot tea and sandwiches. Then, crammed into the back of an old truck with about ten others, they were bumped along miles of road, stopping at German check points and a town filled with German soldiers, but miraculously escaping discovery. A few hours were spent hidden in haystacks near Landeda and then rescue seemed imminent. They were told that there would be a walk along a beach to a rock where they would be picked up by boat.

The long walk brought some surprises, unpleasant ones. In Harold's words, "Once out in the sand the first thing I saw was a big, flat orange object - a land mine with a pencil-sized trigger sticking up from its center. That gets the adrenalin moving." Once free of the mined area there was about a mile to go under the watchful eyes of the Germans manning gun positions above the beach. They were guided by a small group of local men, M. Le Guen, a coastguard officer and some boatmen, who instructed the airmen to pretend to be picking up seaweed and shellfish as the local people did. Once they reached the large rock, which formed part of the island of Tariec at high tide, they found a fisherman, Job Mouden, with a small boat who ferried them, a few at a time, hidden under a pile of lobster crates, to Guenioc, another off-shore island. When they had all been

Men who Dared Death

landed they were told to stay hidden until nightfall when they would be taken to a boat that would come in close to the island. "We couldn't believe our luck. Tomorrow we would be safely in England." They were to be disappointed. It was to be another month before any of them would be safe.

Ile Guenioc and Ile Tariec showing the strand of sand that the escaping airmen had to cross. (D. Carter)

The failure of the pick up on that night of 3-4 November 1943 was due to bad communications. MGB 318 had duly set out from Coastlines Wharf at Falmouth just before five o'clock in the afternoon. One hour later the French radio operator, Jeannot, broadcast the pre-arranged message to London, which the BBC repeated at the end of the evening news to indicate that the operation was on. As long as the weather held and the Germans did not make things awkward, all should be well. However, the men were on one island and the MGB had instructions to go to a different one, and so they returned to Falmouth disappointed.

Harold and the other airmen were left on an uninhabited island, cold, thirsty and hungry and soon very wet in a chill November rain. For three days they stayed there, eating only limpets prised off the rocks and drinking from a shallow depression used by sheep. Eventually Job Mouden and his brother saw them still there and reported back to "Mao". Some bread, wine and blankets were brought to them at great risk in full view of the German look-outs and then "Mao" arranged for them to be ferried back

Men who Dared Death

to the mainland by night and taken in the old truck to the Château of Kerouartz at Lannilis, where they were cheered by a roaring fire and pots of steaming stew. They must have looked a wild lot, because the women who had prepared this, Mme de la Marnière and Mlle Virot, disappeared quickly, afraid for their safety with a bunch of uncivilised men.

The Château of Kerouartz. (D. Carter)

The following day they were given clean clothes, soap and razors and told of a fishing boat that had been bought by the Résistance, which could take six of them to England. So back to the mines and the beach and the rock, this time with some food and drink, but again there was only disappointment as no boat arrived; the fisherman had changed his mind.

Unknown to them another rescue voyage was made from Falmouth in the last week of November when there was no moon. MGB 318 arrived off the coast but found no-one waiting to be picked up because the message had not got through to the French organisation. An SOE agent was dropped off, but again the boat returned having failed in its main mission.

Harold and Rollie were spending this time in a "safe" apartment in Brest with a known collaborator below them and a German major on the floor above. Although they were unable to go out they played chess with their host, Colonel Scheidhauer, and were visited by many people, including girls wanting to learn how to jitterbug.

Men who Dared Death

The area of Brittany where all these rescue attempts were being made was in the far west, in the L'Aber Wrac'h Estuary, full of rocky islands, strong currents and hidden reefs. Navigation was difficult enough under the best of conditions, but in the dark without lights and with the need for complete secrecy, the problems multiplied, and if on top of all this the weather was bad, then the situation could become impossibly dangerous. This became all too obvious at the beginning of December when the third rescue attempt was made.

Once again MGB 318 slipped out of Falmouth in the late afternoon, but this time she was accompanied by a second boat, MGB 329, because of the growing number of people waiting to be picked up. They collected supplies from an SOE launch off the Helford and then crossed to the Breton coast, plunging through the water in an increasing wind. Waves were crashing on the rocks as they negotiated the channel with care in a very black night and then anchored off the little island, Guenioc, where the Americans had waited in vain a month earlier. This time the Americans had not been ferried across there but had been told to stay by the large rock of Tariec, so "Mao" paddled out in a canoe to try and contact the gunboat. Harold Thompson had helped transport this heavy, wooden canoe, carrying it through the fields and heaving it over hedges.

Meanwhile three boats were launched from the MGBs to go to Guenioc, where they found no-one, but then a flashing red light took them to Tariec where twenty desperate men were waiting. Violent wind and rain now made the conditions so appalling that the laden boats could only make headway back to the MGBs with great difficulty. David Birkin, the navigating officer waiting anxiously on board 318, heard the howling in the rigging and saw "great waves rolling in from the Atlantic smashing themselves on to the reefs. The sea was a mass of foam.....It was a most awe-inspiring and frightening sight."

They could not see any of the small boats returning, so after waiting for as long as they dared they decided to up-anchor. Just as they were turning away one of the dinghies was sighted, scarcely moving and with seas breaking over her. The rowers were exhausted and the others were frantically trying to bail out the water, not helped by a leak in the bottom, into which the MGB officer, Lieutenant Uhr-Henry, had stuffed his cap. The gunboat eased its way towards her and lowered the scrambling nets over the side. Three very relieved naval men and seven escapers were dragged on board. One of these was Harold Thompson.

The journey back to Britain was possibly the roughest crossing ever made by MGBs. David Birkin described how "lashings parted and heavy objects started rocketing across the deck - the chart room became chaotic. The table was an indescribable mess of rusty water cascading down the

Men who Dared Death

voice pipe, sick and blood from the bashings of my head against every kind of projection." It was not until early evening that the two boats finally reached the safety of Falmouth Harbour. For Harold Thompson his tour of duty was finished and he could return home to the States. For the crew it was just part of the routine and they would return to Brittany again.

Amazingly no-one died on that dreadful night. The men from the other two small boats managed to reach the comparative safety of the rocky islands and then the problems began all over again for the French. Seven of the airmen had been rescued, but there were still thirteen left, plus two agents and now six members of the boats' crews.

Victor Williams, 2nd from left and P.O. Jim Coles on the right, both members of the crew of MGB 329 who were finally rescued on Christmas Day. (V. Williams)

Transport arrangements must have been a nightmare for the French. Jean-François Derrien, a policeman, organised much of this and he, like all the other Résistance workers, was only too aware of the penalties if the Germans discovered his activities. In his police station was the official notice:

Any Frenchman giving help to enemy aircrews will be shot instantly.

The five naval men were conspicuous in their uniforms, which added to the difficulties of transporting them, but somehow they were all shepherded back into safe houses. Derrien writes, "Everything went well for 'Sarol' and me; no road blocks and no check points. The two post bags were also

Men who Dared Death

saved and left at my house in the woodshed covered over with logs. Luck was with us because that very afternoon roadblocks were set up after the Germans had discovered the surf boats."

Victor Williams (one of the crew from MGB 329) was taken to Brest, where he, his two mates and some of the American airmen stayed in an upstairs flat for the next three weeks. "People were always coming and going," he says, "some bringing food, others news and information. One of the girls often came in the evenings to talk with us and play cards."

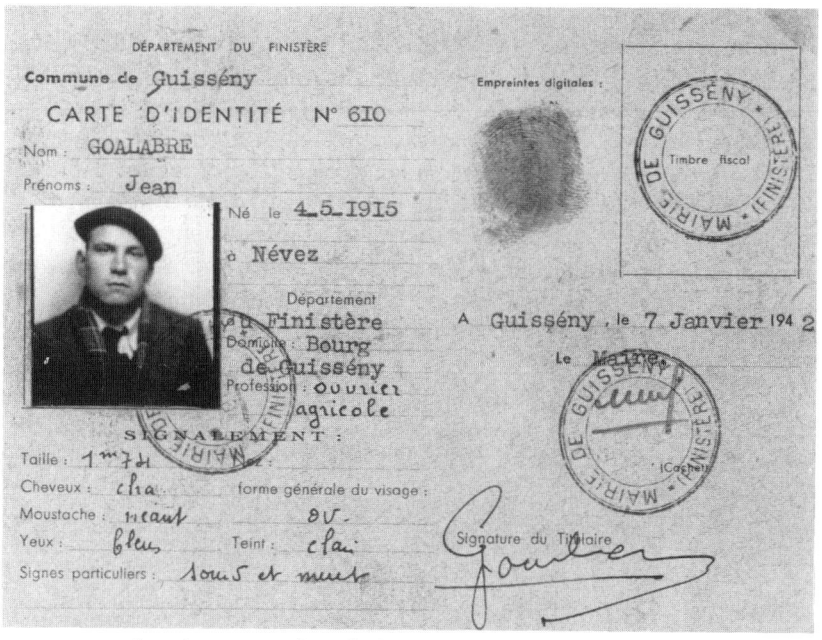

False identity card made for Michael Pollard. (M. Pollard)

Michael Pollard, a lieutenant from MGB 318, was the senior naval officer, and he had a much busier time. He was taken to Paris to be ready for return by air on an arranged Lysander pick-up. He stayed in a small flat, was given suitable clothes and "was taken out nearly every day by one or other of the agents, whose kindness and consideration to me was really wonderful." However the weather was too bad for the air operation, so he returned to Brittany by night train ready for the next rescue attempt by MGB 318.

This started two days before Christmas. The escapers had a hectic five mile walk clambering over hedges and jumping muddy ditches to reach the beach and the large rock of Tariec, escorted by "Mao", M. Le Guen, the coastguard, and two of his friends. The MGB duly arrived off shore as the

45

Men who Dared Death

wind increased to Force 5. Two dinghies were launched with Lieutenant Uhr-Henry and the crew in the first towing the second one behind them. Then the rising seas and wind made it impossible for them to reach the land and they were forced to turn back. In David Birkin's words, "I shall never forget the next quarter of an hour. We could just see the dinghy struggling to reach the MGB - great waves were breaking over her. Tassy (Uhr-Henry) and his crew pulled for their lives as wave after wave broke over the sinking dinghy. By 04.38 they had made it and were hauled aboard, battered and exhausted."

For the stranded escapers and their helpers there was by now the familiar dangerous procedure of returning and splitting up into groups for accommodation, at the Château of Kerouatz and in various houses mainly in Lannilis. Michael Pollard, with a British agent and an RAF pilot, was taken to a farm where they "shared a stable with a very windy horse." But the wait for the next rescue attempt was short. Almost immediately they were being returned to Landeda and then to the beach and the rock in small groups. By the time they were all assembled, the party consisted of about thirty people and so much secret correspondence that it had to be brought by horse and cart. This was the evening of Christmas Day.

Outhouse of M. Le Guen, where airmen hid waiting for rescue. (D. Carter)

Men who Dared Death

It was not only the aircrews and naval men who were expecting to be picked up but also the radio operator, Jeannot, who was planning to escape to Britain. He said to Derrien, "If all goes well, I will transmit a message from London to you. 'Jean-Maurice saved the prestige of the French Police'."

Across the Channel in Falmouth, the crew of the MGB were tired and full after their Christmas dinner of turkey and plum pudding, so it was not with any great eagerness that they responded to the telephone call from London to say that the operation was on for that night. About four o'clock in the afternoon the boat left her moorings and sailed out across the bay, the only boat on the move that day. At the mouth of the Helford they picked up a volunteer crew of SOE men as well as Lieutenant John Garnett,* who had the job of supervising the towing of a twenty-foot surf boat across the Channel. These boats had been tested in heavy surf at Praa Sands for safer landings on the rough shores.

This time the crossing was calm, the landfall was as accurate as usual and they dropped anchor a few hundred yards from where the waiting men were watching anxiously. Everything went like clockwork. "Mao" was able to make contact with the MGB by portable radio, all the men were ferried to the boat, including Michael Pollard and Victor Williams, and

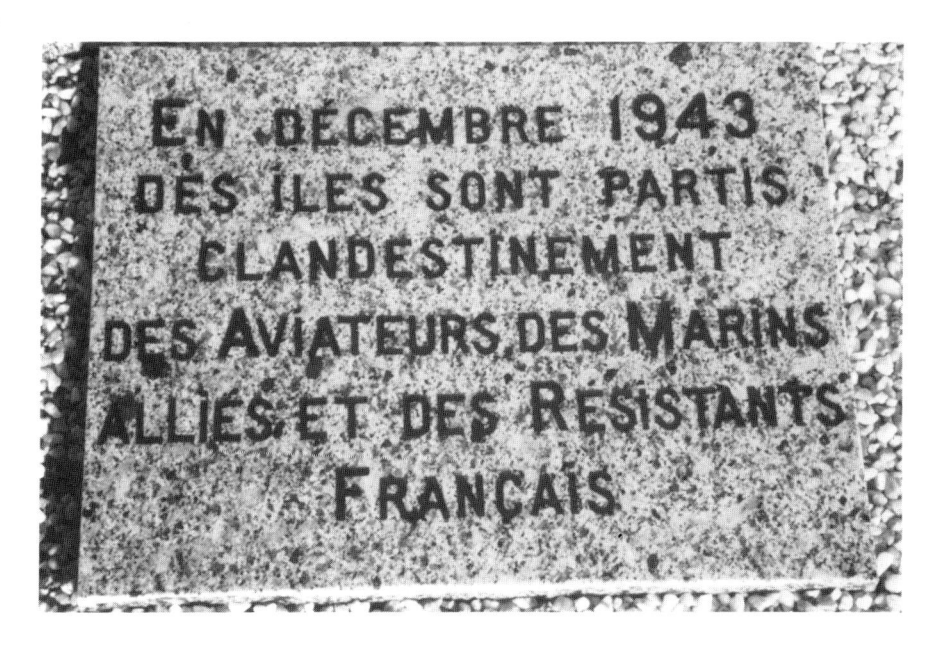

Plaque on the Stele at Landeda, commemorating the Christmas Rescue. (D. Carter)

Men who Dared Death

secret information on the V1 and V2 rocket sites was taken on board with the rest of the huge amount of mail.

On 30 December the BBC from London broadcast the message, "Jean-Maurice saved the prestige of the French Police." Derrien then knew that they had all arrived safely. This story ended happily, but for many Frenchmen who did so much to make escapes like this possible, there was capture, imprisonment, torture, and for some, death. "Mao" (Pierre Hentic) and "Sarol" (Pierre Jeanson), both survived imprisonment in Buchenwald.

Nearly fifty years later Jean-François Derrien received a letter from the First Sea Lord expressing his thanks and gratitude for "your work during these difficult and dangerous years." He concludes, "I am delighted .....to tell you that the details of your inestimable contribution to the Allied war effort have been entered in the appropriate records of the Admiralty."

In August 1994 there was a ceremony at Landeda where a Stele was unveiled to commemorate the liberation of the area, and to recognise the work of the Christmas Rescue team.

In front of the new Stele at Landeda, August 1994.
L. to R. Jean François Derrien, Pierre Jeanson ("Sarol"), Jane Birkin (daughter of David), Préfect, Pierre Hentic ("Mao"), Judy Birkin (wife of David), Harold Thompson. (D. Carter)

4. WOMEN AT WAR

Women at War

George Wingate, the Gunnery Officer for the Port of Falmouth, who would give the signal for firing when air raids over the Docks were imminent, was also involved with the activities based on the Helford, and on occasions crossed over to Brittany on some of the secret operations. The Ferry Boat Inn at Helford Passage, patronised by these officers, was a favourite port of call for him and his Wren fiancée, Pat Donald.

Pat was typical of many young women who were involved in the war effort from the earliest days before conscription began. She was in Plymouth then, working in a busy cake shop during the day but spending her evenings as a part-time ambulance driver, negotiating the narrow streets during the night-time blackout. She had driven ever since she was seventeen and enjoyed it. When she returned to her home in Falmouth, she spent one week in the army, but then, because of her love of vehicles and driving, she was allowed to opt out to join the navy, as soon as transport became included in Wrens' duties.

Falmouth was a port where convoys would arrive roughly every fortnight. Information might have been gained on their voyages of use to the military authorities, so Pat would drive down to the Docks to meet the Signalman and then take officers from the vessels, with their confidential books, to Forte I, on the sea front, now the Membly Hall Hotel, where the Port Admiral had his office.

The vehicles she drove had to use the petrol that was coloured blue, which was to reduce the possibility of its illicit use, as all fuel was in short supply and only available to certain categories of people. There were other occasions when she drove working parties to Padstow and Fowey, when jobs needed to be done, such as seeing to the boom defences that protected harbours. On one occasion she recalls seeing tracer bullets, as she was driving back from Truro, and she remembers the horrifying devastation of Plymouth after bombing. It was almost impossible to recognise her route in the city, as all the familiar landmarks seemed to have disappeared.

Pat was married to George Wingate in July 1942. Weddings during these years of rationing and coupons were difficult. The tiered effect of the cake could be created by cardboard, and a long, white wedding dress worn once only was an extravagance which clothes coupons would not allow. Pat's wedding dress was of turquoise for the ceremony at Budock Church and most of their friends were in uniform. The newspaper account describes her as "well-known and exceedingly popular in Falmouth and a keen golf and hockey player."

As the war continued, women played an increasingly vital role, taking on a wide variety of responsibilities both in and out of the home, from caring for evacuee children, billetting service people, preserving food, "making do and mend" to conserve the country's resources, providing food

Women at War

Pat Wingate with working party, HMS Forte. *(P. Wingate)*

Marriage of Pat and George Wingate. Group includes Wren drivers Nancy Hope and Mary Hough. *(P. Wingate)*

Women at War

drink and shelter in emergencies, running canteens, collecting salvage, organising money-raising for weapons and armaments; to the making of munitions, repairing aeroplanes, working on farms, fire watching, doing observation watches to report on enemy activities - the list seems endless. Some of this was done on a voluntary basis but there were also government campaigns to get women to come forward to fill the vital jobs in industry and the auxiliary services. By 1943 the situation was becoming increasingly desperate and compulsory part-time civilian work was brought in for many women between the ages of eighteen and forty-five.

Conscription of single women between the ages of twenty and thirty for war work began earlier, in December 1941. They could do vital jobs on the farms in the Women's Land Army*, go into the police or fire services, or go into the armed forces. Most were seen at first as doing the clerical work which would release men for the more active roles, but before long, as Pat Wingate experienced, their tasks expanded to cover a much greater variety.

Some, like Pat, became drivers or despatch riders, some were trained to crew anti-aircraft guns as bombing raids caused increasing devastation, some flew planes to transport them from the factories to the airfields where they were so desperately needed, some worked in boats charting the rivers and coasts and helping mine-layers and some had charge of boats in the ports to communicate between shore and the fighting ships. When the war began there were only half a dozen or so types of jobs available to Wrens, but by 1945 this had risen to nearly one hundred.

It was seeing a motor launch manned by Wrens in Falmouth, that made Barbara Lorentzen (née Kneebone) try to join the service when she was only sixteen. The sea was in her blood, having been born of a boating family and brought up in a waterfront cottage, close to boatyards and beaches of the town. This was the sort of job she wanted and not to be stuck behind a desk. Her persistence and qualifications got her into the Wrens under age. She spent much of her time in Dartmouth where she managed a motor launch, taking personnel from shore to ship, but there were times when she was posted back to her home town.

Secret raids were made from Falmouth across the Channel to Western France, the most famous of these being in March 1942 when a combined commando/naval expedition left for St Nazaire, on the estuary of the Loire, to destroy the huge dry dock there.* Most of the boats used for this enterprise were the small, powerful motor launches, used for coastal defence, whose base in Falmouth. with motor gun boats and motor torpedo boats, was at Coastlines Wharf, near the entrance to the Penryn River.

These boats were often worked to the limit of their capabilities and needed repairing and careful checking. Maintenance men would be

Women at War

regularly picked up from Customs House Quay and taken by boat to HMS Forte IV, as this base was known, to work on the boats during the day and then they would be returned in the late afternoon. This ferry service was provided by a Wren boatcrew, one of the boats used being a Falmouth Quay Punt, *Moyanna*.

Barbara Kneebone with Joyce Mumford on the stern of *Moyanna*, Trot Boat for Coastal Forces, HMS Forte. *(B. Lorentzen)*

When Barbara was working in Falmouth, her duties would start at 08.00, taking the trot boat, *Moyanna*, across to Flushing to pick up naval staff and maintenance men and return them to Custom House Quay. Then it was on to Coastlines Wharf, where maintenance men were dropped and men and mail collected to be taken to the Dockyards. Here, in one corner, was YC5, a green barge, of which little was known or spoken about, where she picked up secret signals. If supplies were needed in the Dockyards then she would take them there, and in the afternoon personnel would need to be ferried back to the quay and to Flushing.

Women at War

Much as she loved this there were dangers involved especially from air attacks. She won recognition for her bravery when boats were hit in Dartmouth,* and on one occasion in Falmouth, as she was going to the Docks, a German plane came over flying low, which set all the guns on the ships in the Docks firing at it. She heard a swooshing noise and then saw that the standard flag, flying on the stern, was holed by their shrapnel.

The failure or success of individual war operations could depend, as shown in the secret operations in Brittany, on good communications, and women were involved in many aspects, as telephonists, radio telegraphers, cipher clerks and radar operators and plotters. (Chapter 6) This last job could take them away from the desks and screens and into the air. Some Wrens flew regularly to calibrate radar equipment, and Judy McSwiney, a Wren based at St Merryn, recalls one who was resourceful enough to use her metal lipstick holder as a substitute fuse for the wireless transmitter. On another occasion a plane with Wrens on board flew close to a Liberator. The Wrens, peering out of the window, saw from the shocked faces of the American crew, that women on board were a completely unexpected sight.

The communications building on many a station was the protected centre of activity. Judy McSwiney worked for three years in the PBC (Protected Communications Building) at RNAS St Merryn, or HMS Vulture, as it was known. She had joined the services before conscription began and arrived there in early 1941, working at first in the telephone exchange, with 140 extensions which had to be learnt by heart. There were also special lines which one "blew" down to the Flag Officer, Naval Air Stations at Lee-on-Solent. She recalls, "We discovered, by unplugging we could make toast on it!"

She found that the concentration required was exhausting, especially at the beginning, when she had to learn to attach cords from the caller to the called, hold about five different people at once, all requiring individual requests like trunk calls and directory enquiries, and ring each number by hand. "Yellow lights showed when people were talking and flashed impatiently when reconnection was required."

She remembers the time when air raids were a constant menace. The first warning, a Red Alert, would come through from RAF St Eval nearby, and then Purple meant that a raid was imminent. The Wren on duty at the telephone exchange sounded the siren to warn the personnel on the station to take shelter, although Wrens on watch would remain at their posts. Constant night-time raids, allowing little sleep, took their toll, not helped by the impossibility of proper rest when off duty during the day, with the Wren Stewards "banging around the hut with their brooms and dustpans, accompanied by renderings of 'Amapola' and 'I Don't Want to Set the World on Fi-er'."

Women at War

The "Wrennery" at RNAS St Merryn today. (J. McSwiney)

After one bad raid the Wrens returned to their quarters to find they had been hit, and they had to sleep with most of the windows and one wall blown out, "and curious sailors, intrigued by slumbering Wrens." As a result of the bombing the Wrens' quarters were transferred to the Treglos Hotel, Constantine Bay, "where eight of us shared the bare-boarded 'best-suite', alleged to have been occupied by the Duke of Windsor."

Judy was promoted to the Signals Distributing Office (SDO), where the immediate pressures were not so intense but the responsibility was greater. Here she had to deal with signals, "either in plain language, teleprinter, W/T(wireless/telegraphy), or code." At night, when the Yeoman of Signals was not on duty, the responsibility was the Wrens' as to how and to whom the signals were transmitted. If a secret cypher signal came in, they had to waken the Cypher Officer, who was sleeping nearby. Each night the Secret Coding books had to be checked by the Duty Commanding Officer and SDO Wren, and if any of the books was mislaid, the coding would have to be changed all over the world.

Night duty ended at 08.00 hours, but an hour before then the Wrens had to clean out the offices and polish the table tops and floors before being transported back to their accommodation at Constantine. "If Yeo, our boss, found a trace of dirt even high up on the window ledges, he would send for us and we would wake from our fitful day slumbers and have to bike back the two miles and do the job again."

Women at War

Wireless/telegraphy room, RNAS St Merryn. *(J. McSwiney)*

The signals that came in covered a wide variety of subjects, including details on spare parts for the planes, meteorological reports and the time of take off for planes, their destination and their estimated time of arrival. "We dreaded the 'plane overdue' signals."

One evening, when Judy was on duty, the Padstow Coastguard telephoned to report a plane that had crashed into the sea. She rang the RAF Sea Rescue Unit and informed the various officers on site and in the end all was well. The pilot was able to swim the mile to the shore, but for most of that way he had to support his gunner who was unable to swim.

On one occasion she helped in the "capture" of the Captain of HMS Vulture. Commandos were training at the station, when the threat of a German invasion was still strong. Their Commander felt that the airfield was far too vulnerable to capture and wanted to prove this to the Captain. The plan involved the use of the station switchboard, and with the connivance of the Wren Officer in charge, Judy was the chosen operator.

Women at War

She sneaked out of the hotel late at night, where she met up with the Commandos, and found the Wrens' usual transport bus ready to take them to the airfield. The Marine on guard duty gave the driver and bus a cursory look, before waving it on, while the passengers were hiding, crouching down in complete silence.

The exchange was "captured" complete with the Wrens who were on duty, and the control tower taken over with no trouble. Judy then rang the Captain, and following instructions, told him that he was urgently needed at the guard house. On his arrival he was promptly "imprisoned" and the point was proved.

Wren on duty in the Control Tower, St Merryn. (J. McSwiney)

"The war could not have been won without the magnificent efforts of the women of Britain." This was said by Queen Elizabeth at a special gathering in London of women's representatives from all parts of the country. The war had not even finished then, because this meeting was held in December 1944, when some of the civilian war organisations were already being stood down or being put on to a reduced peace-time footing.

Over the next few months many of those in the women's armed forces began to join the ranks of civilians, wondering if the skills they had learned in war would now be valued in peace time. Some, like Barbara Lorentzen, found that although she was still only twenty-one, her

Women at War

qualifications enabled her to gain a Waterman's licence, so that she could skipper a boat up the Fal, in the bay and harbour and along the coast, the only woman at that time to do so. But not all were able to adapt to civilian life so easily.

Barbara Kneebone having a farewell drink with the crews of the Fal Quay Punts at the Pandora Inn 1945. (B. Lorentzen)

5. LINES AROUND THE WORLD

One night, three hundred Scottish infantrymen arrived at an isolated cove near Land's End. By dawn they had started their work. The beautiful white beach was sealed off by barbed wire and an unscalable floodlit fence, tank traps were dug in case of an invasion by sea, and artillery was hidden in "haystacks". Pill boxes were built on the cliffs above the sands, and a guard post was set up on the one road that led down to the cove, with the way barred to all those without passes. This cove, isolated though it was, held the key to Britain's communications with her Empire and much of the world, and its defence was vital. It was Porthcurno, or PK as it was known to the company of Cable and Wireless that operated it.

Porthcurno had been a telegraph cable station since 1870. In that year the Falmouth-Gibraltar Cable Company had laid a cable from Gibraltar, through Lisbon and on to Britain, where it was brought ashore at Porthcurno, whose soft shell-sand beach and shelter from westerly gales, made an ideal site. A small school for operators was also established, the forerunner of the Engineering College. In the following years other cables were laid here, until by 1928 there were fourteen, and it was regarded as the most important cable station in the British Empire.

Porthcurno had also gained early experience with radio technology, although this was strictly unofficial. Soon after the turn of the century, Marconi had astounded his detractors by making wireless contact across the miles of ocean to Newfoundland. His experiments had taken place on the far side of Mount's Bay from Porthcurno, on the cliffs above Poldhu Cove on the Lizard Peninsula. This possible competition from newer technology worried the cable operators, who set up a "listening post" on the cliffs above Porthcurno, in distant view of Marconi's masts. With the use of their 170 foot high receiver mast they were able to eavesdrop on Marconi's progress. In 1928 there was an amalgamation of many of the rival telegraph and wireless companies and the new company that emerged became known as Cable and Wireless Ltd.

This company owned nearly half of all the cables in the world, while the Germans had only two, one to Lisbon and the other to the Azores, both of which were cut on the afternoon of 3 September 1939 on the declaration of war. Cables had one big advantage over radio communication and that was privacy: communication by cable could not be tapped by the enemy.

Lines around the World

Obviously the enemy could also cut British cables, but this did not happen until Italy joined the war in 1940, when the five cables that formed the direct link with the Middle East, Far East, India and Australia were cut. In spite of this, it was still possible to pass messages by other routes, although the diversions were thousands of miles longer.

Action was quickly taken to protect the London end of the operations, but the company also had five more stations around the country. The one at Bodmin was taken over by the Air Ministry, but if the others were all put out of action, the plan was to transfer all surviving equipment to Porthcurno. This seemed to be the safest area until the fall of France in June 1940, when Cornwall became more vulnerable than many other places. It was then that Porthcurno was made as impregnable against attack as possible.

The valley that runs down to the beach is steep, and two tunnels were blasted into the hill on the eastern side, which were connected in the middle and became known just as "the Tunnel". Two hundred Cornish tin miners, with experts from Ireland and Yorkshire, began this huge job on 25 June 1940, and all through that summer and autumn the valley shook with thunderous explosions as 15,000 tons of granite were blasted away. Each tunnel was 110 feet long (later increased to 150 feet), 26 feet wide and 23 feet high.

A small railway was built to remove the piles of debris that were so large they were changing the contours of the valley sides. Nets were used at first as a safety precaution against flying rocks, but this protection was soon ignored as speed became more essential than safety. Windows of nearby houses shattered, gaping holes appeared in roofs and there was nearly a tragedy when one huge boulder was hurled through the manager's kitchen window, but luckily neither he nor his wife was in at the time.

Speculation amongst local people was rife, but did they believe the story told them that a short cut was being made to the Logan Rock Inn a mile away?

Once the tunnels had been blasted out, the next crowd of workmen moved in. Water-proofers sealed the floors, roofs and walls, plasterers covered the walls, electricians installed a maze of wiring, wood and brick offices were built inside the tunnels for the instruments, generators, batteries, wireless receivers and other paraphernalia. In spite of the precautions, damp proved to be a problem at first with fungus developing, until air-conditioning dried out the atmosphere. It was then found that with a steady temperature, no vibrations and little dust, the speed of the circuits actually increased.

Massive blast-proof doors of steel an inch thick protected the entrances, to make this like an impregnable fortress. In addition rubber

Lines around the World

gaskets were fitted on the inside as a protection against poison gas. However, the cable operators were at work here before these were completed, so tarpaulins covered the entrances at first, while the people sitting at their tables shivered in their overcoats. In case these huge doors jammed, trapping the workers inside, 119 narrow steps led steeply upwards through the granite rock at the back of the tunnel to emerge on to the hillside above.

Instrument Room in the Tunnel. (Cable & Wireless)

Additional defence was provided by a Bofors gun, and a battery of rocket projectors mounted outside, and most sinister of all were the flame throwers that protected the beach and the two entrances. This system of defence was set up where sites were especially important and Porthcurno was not the only place in Cornwall where this method was used; the entrance to the Helford River was also protected by a flame barrage, which made an awesome sight when tested.* At Porthcurno, the tanks for holding the petrol and oil were built into the valley sides above the tunnels, where pipes could bring the lethal mixture down the hill side.

In May 1941 the new communication centre was officially opened by the chairman's wife, Lady Wilshaw, with the job completed in less than a year.

Lines around the World

Plans had to be made in case the enemy landed at Porthcurno and took over the station, in spite of all these defensive precautions. The first line of defence would be the infantry based at the station and two men were constantly on guard at the tunnel entrances. These were often tough Scottish soldiers, the Black Watch and Gordon Highlanders, but the Inniskillens are remembered as being the wildest of the troops. Secret code words would alert the branch managers further along the cable chains if enemy takeover seemed imminent, but the equipment would have to be destroyed or made inoperable rather than let it fall into enemy hands for their use. In case of attack or siege, food and other provisions were stored in the tunnel, a first-aid post was set up and staff formed themselves into a Home Guard platoon.

Military police were also on guard there and on one occasion when bombs fell nearby, staff enjoying some fresh air outside were bundled by them into the tunnel and the huge doors were slammed behind them. Several bombs fell in the area, one near miss happening when the German aircraft seemed to be aiming for the nearby meteorological station, but it was usually the fields that suffered, which was annoying for the farmers, but less vital to the nation.

The station was operating day and night, with the staff working a four-shift day; in the morning from eight o'clock to one, then the afternoon shift worked until seven o'clock, the evening shift until midnight and then there was an eight-hour shift until the following morning. In emergencies this might need to be changed. Bombs could destroy land lines and on one occasion, when lines near Bristol had been wrecked, breaking the link with London, eight-hour shifts were worked for a week or more, and all the messages had to be taken by couriers to London on the train from Penzance.

Staff had to be easily available to be on duty on time, whatever the changed circumstances, and some were billeted in the nearby farms, where living conditions were not always ideal. One man recalls the lack of a bath, and so the manager's house had to supply this facility.

Although Porthcurno remained relatively unscathed by the war, the operators could see for themselves enemy and allied activities along the coast, with convoys passing, some being attacked by torpedoes or bombs as E-boats lurked near the shores and planes roared overhead. Along the cables and through their offices passed the doleful news of defeat and retreat. Cable and Wireless lost not only their branches in Europe at Amsterdam, Antwerp, Paris and then Athens, but the Japanese advances in the east, to Singapore, Hong Kong, Manila, the East Indies (Indonesia), meant that all these cable stations were put out of action. In northern Australia, bombing raids on Darwin forced the station there to be

Lines around the World

A sentry guards the entrance to the Tunnel. *(Cable & Wireless)*

Lines around the World

dismantled when further attacks seemed imminent, but luckily no invasion followed.

Gradually the news became brighter and, as 1944 dawned, the momentum was building up for the final showdown, the opening of the second front and the invasion of German-occupied Europe. The success of this eventually brought to an end the war in Europe and then the Allies concentrated on the last enemy, Japan.

The Thin Red Line by Charles Graves, which tells the story of Cable and Wireless during the war, opens with these comments. "Without cable and wireless, the Big Three could never have encompassed the destruction of the Axis. .... Momentous campaigns, which would previously have taken two years, were completed in six weeks. .... All which was largely due to the immensely stepped-up speed of communications - radio being essential for the tactical handling of troops and cables for strategy." Porthcurno had played a vital part in this.

As the war was drawing slowly towards its end there was some relaxation of security at the station, with Italian prisoners of war living in

An engineer at work in the Tunnel. (Cable & Wireless)

Lines around the World

the area of the Engineering College and allowed to walk around, guarded by soldiers of the Duke of Cornwall's Light Infantry (DCLI). Cable and Wireless was already preparing for the re-opening of their stations in the Far East.

Training was underway for young men to take over as each area was liberated, because the employees who had been imprisoned were not expected to be in a fit condition to start work again immediately. Some of the men were with the advancing Allied soldiers, where they were able to despatch the reports of war correspondents close to the front line, in spite of very difficult conditions. The stations at Rangoon, Singapore, Hong Kong, all opened up again, sometimes when the Japanese were still officially in control. Their messages once more were relayed on to Porthcurno.

As Allied troops closed in on Japan, the war came to an end more abruptly than many had dared to hope, with the first use of atomic weapons. Now people in Britain were desperate for news of family and friends who might have survived their ordeals. And Cable and Wireless obliged. Before the end of August 1945, the *West Briton* reported that there were arrangements for free telegrams to be sent across the world. Released prisoners would be able to send home a telegram free of charge and a prepaid reply form would be sent to each recipient, courtesy of the company.

Today this popular cove still has its strategic importance. It is still the landfall for international cables and in late 1996 the longest-ever marine cable, linking Porthcurno with Japan, will become operative. The secret wartime communications complex is secret no longer, although red tape over the Official Secrets Act has precluded the inclusion of employees' memories of that time. The Tunnel has now been opened to the public, so far on a restricted basis: Thursdays and Fridays in 1995, and it is hoped every day in the season from 1996. Amongst the historic equipment on display going back to the early days of telegraphy communication, people can now see and wonder at the emergency measures taken to protect these vital lines of communication during those years of war.

Details on the opening times for the Tunnel can be obtained from the Chief Executive of the Trevithick Trust, Mr Stuart Smith, 01209 612142.

6. RADAR - THE SECRET WEAPON

The Lizard Peninsula, with its prehistoric burial mounds, early Christian crosses and rare plants on the isolated downs, seems an unlikely area to play a prominent part in the war, but its position is of strategic importance. This is shown today by the strange collection of satellite tracking dishes towering over the heath on Goonhilly Downs, and here in 1940 when Falmouth suddenly became vulnerable to air attacks from the German forces in France, a mobile radar station was rushed, to detect low-flying enemy aircraft as they crossed the Channel.

Radar was a vital weapon, the knowledge of which was highly secret. RAdio Detection And Ranging, using radio waves to locate distant objects, was being developed in Britain during the 1930s, based on the work of earlier scientists. Experiments had been made in America, Germany and Britain for some years, but it was the threat of war that boosted research.

In 1934 Robert Watson-Watt, a Scottish scientist, pointed out to the newly set-up Air Ministry Committee under Sir Henry Tizard the possibility of detecting aeroplanes in flight, and he was later able to give a successful demonstration of this. As a result, a chain of radio location stations was built around the south and east coasts. It was thought unnecessary to include Cornwall in this radar "curtain" at first, but by the late summer of 1940 three had been set up: on Rame Head to protect Plymouth, at Carnanton close to the airfield of St Eval, and at Dry Tree on Goonhilly Downs.

The first radar station here at Dry Tree was mobile, using small aerials on vans that could detect planes approaching up to thirty miles away flying at 1,000 feet. This used the Chain Home Low (CHL) system, a "beam-type" radar with a rotatable aerial. But before long a more permanent station was built on the Chain Home (CH) system, which had fixed aerials providing "floodlight" cover over a wide area. This was the main component of the British early warning system throughout the war and could detect high-flying planes up to 200 miles away.

At Goonhilly it became a very noticeable feature of the landscape with its four tall, thin, pencil-shaped transmitter towers over 300 feet high supporting the wires. These towers were of a simpler design than those used at the earlier stations further east and this type of aerial array was known as 'West Coast Array'. At first the towers were arranged in a "V"-shape to give two 'lines of shoot', one south- south- east towards Falmouth

Radar - the Secret Weapon

Typical West Coast CH Station.
(Crown copyright reproduced by permission of the Controller of HMSO.)

and across the Channel to France, and the other west-south-west covering the South-West Approaches. In 1940, when there was an invasion scare in the area, the Coverack Home Guard were ordered to try and prevent the enemy from landing, but if this failed they were to retreat to this radar station and defend it for as long as possible.

Later, after some damaging air raids in the South East, the authorities decided that two separate stations would be better, so a second CH station was built at nearby Trelanvean to cover the Falmouth/Channel area. After that one of Dry Trees' lines of shoot was dismantled. Like the site at Dry Tree, Trelanvean spread over a wide area with two pairs of tall transmitter towers at some distance from the two pairs of shorter receivers. This duplication was to ensure that one was always operative. High winds could sweep across the open heathland, so a bad-weather weight was erected by each mast to give greater flexibility to the wires to prevent breakage. Builders doing completion work on the site helped in rescue work, after a fatal raid on Coverack in August 1942 killed four people, including a four-year-old boy sent there for safety, and injured many more.

The drawback of the CH system was that it could not detect planes flying at a low level, so when it was decided that the mobile low-altitude system at Dry Tree, Goonhilly, was too far from the coast, a permanent CHL station was built close to Lizard Head. This area of Bass Point and

Radar - the Secret Weapon

Pen Olver was already the site of communication installations. Marconi had set up a wireless station here in 1901 and the castellated building on the cliff top, around which the radar buildings were to be installed, was the Lloyd's Signalling Station for communicating to passing vessels, although for security reasons the light signals were stopped during the war.

Base of radar installation at Trelanvean today. (V. Acton)

The new radar site was manned by personnel from all three services. The army provided the guards that were essential for such a secret operation, and even the families and staff of the Signal Station had to show their passes at the gate in the barbed-wire fence. Colin Francis, whose father was the Lloyds Signalmaster here, writes "Morale was very good between the staff and the servicemen and bundles of firewood eagerly changed hands for a hot cup of tea during the cold night guard duties. Two anti-aircraft guns were installed in circular gun pits immediately in front of the Signal Station." He also adds that the "birdcage" radar aerial fixed on top of the old nightbox (housing the morse lamp for signalling at night) "caused the domestic wireless to make a loud hum on every revolution of the aerial."

The primary purpose of the radar station was the reporting by air force personnel of any low-flying enemy planes approaching the area. But this radar, particularly with the improved CHEL (Chain Home Extra Low)

Radar - the Secret Weapon

system, could also detect planes near the surface and even ships. The coasts of Cornwall were menaced by German E boats preying on the convoys and by planes and boats laying mines to prevent the use of Falmouth Harbour, so Wrens were stationed here to report on enemy activity to naval headquarters in Falmouth.

The CHEL system was evolved to counteract the German bombers' attempts to avoid radar detection by slinging a couple of bombs under the fuselage and then flying in at sea level. The transmitter and receiver for this system were both housed in mobile vans, each with a fixed 'cheese' antenna on the top rotated manually. Joan Donkin, who was a radar operator here, remembers that it was very difficult to keep a steady sweep in gale force winds and in these circumstances they would "enlist the brawn of the watch Radar Mechanic on duty."

Weather conditions could make life hazardous. Joan remembers going on watch at times "when we felt our way along the footpath, linked up with each other in the thick fog that often prevailed" and she adds that living so close to the Lizard lighthouse, "where sea mists swept in quite often we would go to sleep and wake up listening to the loud throaty 'boom-wah' of its huge horn".

There was also a fourth radar station in this one small area on the Lizard, at Treleaver, which was a Ground Control Interception (GCI) base. This was a form of radar used to improve the accuracy of night-time fighters trying to shoot down German bombers. It was being tried out by a few squadrons during the early months of 1941 when the success rate improved dramatically.

One pilot, Flight Lieutenant John Cunningham, gained fame for his successes at this time when flying with 604 Squadron which was testing it. After a spectacular shooting down of a Heinkel over South Devon, his third kill in a short time, the newspapers were full of his exploits and were beginning to wonder how he could see in the dark, nick-naming him "Cat's Eyes". To damp down on this speculation of his ability someone thought up the idea of claiming that his amazing night-time vision was the result of eating raw carrots. And so a myth was born that is perhaps still with us today. Anything was preferable to the risk of the secrets of radar being discovered.

The mobile GCI system was installed at Treleaver in June of that year. This consisted of two lorries, each towing trailers with aerials which were operated by two RAF men pedalling as if they were on a bike. In a high wind this could become almost impossible. The first lorry was for the transmitter and towed an aerial about ten feet high. The second one was the Operations Room which held the receiver, cathode ray tubes and a

Radar - the Secret Weapon

plotting table. A third vehicle contained various accessories and towed a generator trailer.

On one side of the Operations Room was an electromagnetic tube, the Plan Position Indicator (PPI), and opposite it was the electrostatic height tube, which had a screen with a split trace. The controller sat in the middle viewing both screens. It was a skilled job to estimate the height of an aircraft. Two sections of the receiver aerial were used for this. The times taken for the radio signal to bounce off the aircraft and return to different parts of the aerial were different, and by measuring this time difference on the screen and taking the range into account, the height could be estimated. This sounds not only complicated but also chancy, but according to two of the people who worked there then, Pamela West and Margaret Diplock, crews became very proficient at using this arrangement.

The other members of the team were: the WAAF operator at the Navigation Board taking account of the winds and cloud height; the recorder who recorded information on the tracing paper over the operational maps; the telephonist who worked the PBX system (Private Branch Exchange); and the teller who kept in touch with Portreath and Predannack airfields.

When the Goonhilly or Trelanvean stations detected from long range on their powerful aerials the approach of hostile planes, they reported to RAF Portreath. Beaufighters fitted with Airborne Radar were then scrambled, usually from Predannack, and Treleaver would make contact with them and guide them towards the enemy.

The pilots had to learn how to use the new equipment. Squadrons newly-posted to the area soon learned the advantages, when they were told to send up a plane and fly at any height, at any speed and in any direction. Within three minutes the radar crew could plot the plane and report to the pilot all this information.

The radar crews were divided into three watches of unequal length, the longest being the night watch from 9 o'clock in the evening to 9 o'clock in the morning. Later the watches were changed to a four-shift system, but it seemed no less tiring for the operators. When night-time enemy raids were the norm the work during the day consisted mainly of practice intercepts and calibration which was very important.

At times there could be unexpected excitement. Peter Boving, a Canadian radar mechanic at Treleaver, remembers one occasion when the Beaufighter crews were doing their usual daytime testing of their engines and aircraft, not under radar control. "The Beaufighters would beat in from the sea at Angels Zero, and shoot up the cliffs and over the roof of the Headland." (This was one of the hotels in Coverack.) He adds "Shoot ups were finally frowned on when a Beau dived at the radar site. The air

Radar - the Secret Weapon

compression during pullout created quite a rainstorm. The observer had idly cleared the gun lock, and the pilot idly flipped the cover and thumbed the trigger and just missed a radar mechanic who was walking from the transmitter to the receiver. Luckily no one was hurt."

Radar mechanics at Treleaver. *(P.West)*

Mechanics and operators on the radar stations were people of vital importance. They could not talk about their work to anyone outside - the word 'radar' was unknown to the general public - and they had the responsibility of preventing the Germans from gaining important information about their systems if there was an attack. Peter Boving recalls that in these circumstances his orders were "to remove the modulators from the transmitter and a cable from the receiver and smash them with a cricket bat". Some of the men believed that the army guards on the site had orders to shoot any radar mechanic if he was threatened with capture by a German raiding party, which was quite possible.

Jack Nissen, who had been involved with radar research at Bawdsey Research Station in Essex before the war, continued this work in the RAF. When, in August 1942, the raid on Dieppe was made by Canadian troops, he was with a smaller group that landed further west at Pourville, to gain information desperately needed by the British authorities, about the German radar station there. The main Dieppe raid was a disaster but in spite of horrendous difficulties and casualties, Jack Nissen was able to reach

Radar - the Secret Weapon

the perimeter of the radar station and cut the wires. This meant that the German operators were forced to communicate by radio transmitter and their messages could be picked up in Britain, so vital technical knowledge was gained. He was one of the few who returned safely, but he knew that the soldiers who acted as a bodyguard for him also had orders to shoot him if he was in danger of capture.

This raid showed to the Allies that a successful invasion of Europe could only be achieved with better navigational aids and equipment and so the race for radar dominance continued with increased activity in Cornwall and elsewhere in the country during the following year.

By Christmas 1942 the Treleaver station had been upgraded to an Intermediate GCI, a wood-framed building with a aerial 35 feet high, which took ten men three days to erect. This aerial acted as both transmitter and receiver and turned in complete circles. The pedal power of the "Turners" was not needed now as it was power-operated. Within a few months a permanent brick and concrete GCI station was built there, the Happidrome as it was called, which had a range of 90 miles for general use and 45 miles for interception.

The conditions were now much more comfortable. The room, partly underground, was large, 160 feet long and 35 feet wide. Four pairs of sets were installed and they could monitor aircraft on different frequencies, which could be a help in rescue work. Margaret Diplock, or Mac as she was known then, remembers one occasion when they saw on their new screens a pilot bale out of his plane close to the French coast, and they watched the blip on the calibration scale of the height tube slide from 600 feet to sea level, as the parachute glided down into the water. They were able to guide the Walrus air-sea rescue plane to within one mile of the place and as she says, "No-one wanted to go off watch until the rescue was complete."

By June 1944 there were at least seventeen different sites around the coasts of Cornwall, including one on the Isles of Scilly at Newford, with the biggest concentrations on the two peninsulas of the Lizard and Land's End. Sennen became an important site for two new radar systems, OBOE and GEE. The first was for precision bombing and the second was a navigational aid for planes which could provide accuracy to within 100 yards. Details of the progress made in establishing them were given in "Most Secret" progress reports from TRE (the Telecommunications Research Establishment, which was moved to Malvern from Swanage after the Bruneval Raid because of fear of reprisals). The first report early in 1943 shows the setting up of the OBOE station.

"As a result of a meeting at Air Ministry the TRE experimental stations at Worth Travers (9011) and West Prawle (9012) have been

Radar - the Secret Weapon

handed over to 60 Group for work as operational stations Type 9000." (60 Group was the RAF's technical division which serviced the radar network, with the local headquarters for the entire South-West at Ashburton in Devon.) "The station at West Prawle has been stripped, the equipment brought up to date at TRE, and re-installed at Sennen (Land's End). Both Worth and Sennen are now equipped for K-Oboe and were technically serviceable on the night of 8th February 1943. A test flight was made on 9th February 1943. Tests on a single frequency have given signals from an aircraft at 250 miles from Sennen."

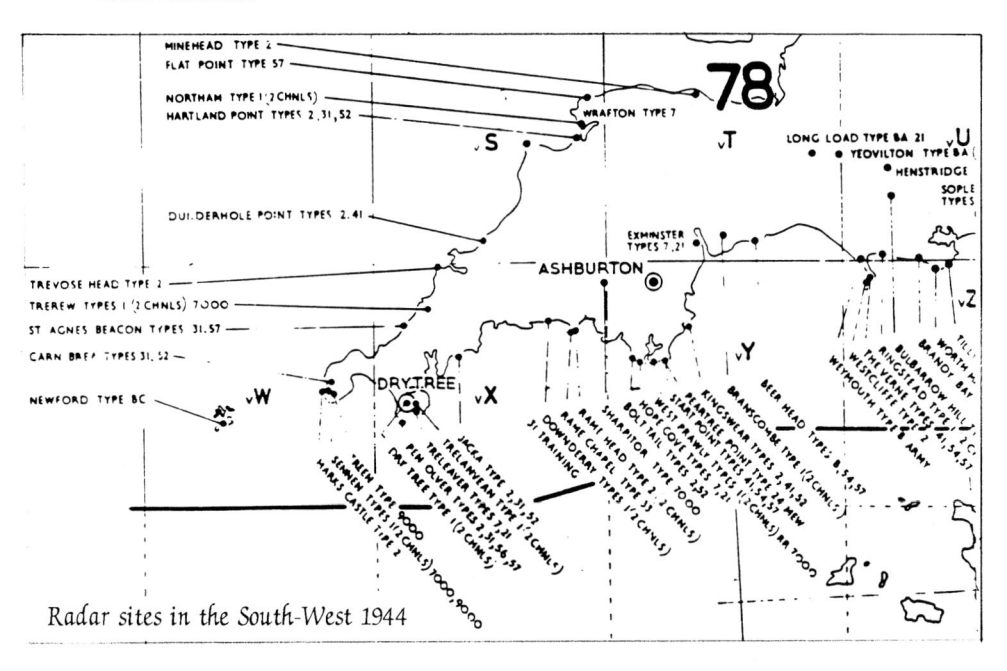

Radar sites in the South-West 1944

The GEE system began to be used first in March 1942 and made possible the 1,000 bomber raids of that year to saturate enemy targets. A year later it was being planned for Sennen, as the following "Most Secret" progress report shows dated March 1943. Under the heading GEE it states:

"A long range flight to Gibraltar and back has been made in order to check the effective ranges of the proposed stations for the South-Western system. At the normal operational height for Coastal Command (1000-2000 ft) maximum range was approximately 300 miles." It later states "Towers redundant to the present CH requirements have been found available at all six stations, (master at

Radar - the Secret Weapon

Sharpitor, slaves at Worth, Sennen and Folly, monitors at West Prawle and Trerew) except at the new master site, where a 240 ft timber tower is required. ......the small amount of new work involved suggests that there should be little difficulty in meeting the target date of mid-June for operations."

When a tall tower was built on the Pen Olver site in 1944, it provoked great debate among the local people. Joan Donkin recalls that "there was much discussion in the village and the general consensus was that it was a giant loudspeaker installed to warn the villagers of any impending invasion."

Radar tower for Pen Olver, behind the Lloyd's Signalling Station. (S. Smith)

Coastal Command at St Eval had to deal with the German menace in the waters around the south-west coasts and planes here were fitted with ASV (Air to Surface Vessel) radar to locate ships at sea. With all these new systems the equipment needed testing and people had to be trained to use them effectively. In August 1943 a team from TRE at Malvern was sent to the air base to check the equipment and help the RAF. Pilots with this equipment had sighted U boats, but the ASV system had failed to register them, so the team had to find out whether it was technical malfunction or pilot error that had caused this. Detailed tests were carried out and in the report, as usual "Most Secret", one of the recommendations was that

Radar - the Secret Weapon

maintenance of good sensitivity "is specialised enough to warrant allocation in particular to only two or three mechanics in each maintenance party."

Most of these radar stations were in very isolated positions, which could make life difficult for the personnel working in them, especially in the early days. Joan Donkin remembers the Nissen huts at Start Point in Devon where the radar operators and mechanics had to live. "There was no running water or flush toilets and they went down to West Prawle for a bath once a week. We could hear the rats running over us between the two layers of metal in the roof." At least on the Lizard most of the personnel had more comfortable accommodation because of the number of hotels in the area that were able to be requisitioned.

WAAF radar operators outside the Headland Hotel, Coverack. (P.West)

Peter Boving, based at Treleaver for some time from Christmas 1941, remembers that WAAF operators were housed at the Headland Hotel on the west side of Coverack, some other personnel were at Channel View, and he as a radio mechanic was at the Paris, which had the only operating bar in the village at that time. "It was as close to being a large family as you could get", he recalls, "with meals eaten in the kitchen. We often helped with washing glasses, or rolling barrels of beer to the bar when the brewery dray came." Here servicemen and locals met and he remembers old Tim who was said not to have had a bath since his wife's funeral. "The warmer weather lent substance to this rumour." They would set up pints

Radar - the Secret Weapon

for him and Tim's response was "Ere's tu ee, an if thaat's not good enuff, ere's tu ee agin!" This situation lasted for all too short a time, because orders came that the airmen should be put under canvas for the summer, so it was Bell tents and a marquee for a mess until he was posted to Dorset.

Just over a year later Joan Donkin was posted to Pen Olver and was accommodated at the Housel Bay Hotel "wonderfully situated overlooking the sea and high up on the cliffs." However they "did not languish in comfy hotel beds. Our iron beds and 3 piece biscuit mattresses were waiting for us along with the scratchy blankets and hard bolster." The women, unlike the men, had the added comfort of sheets and most brought their own soft pillows with them. She also adds "We carried bath plugs with us having learned the first week in the WAAF that no ablutions anywhere were so equipped."

Social life was restricted in an isolated area like this. Peter Boving recalls one Sunday soccer match, "the only outing to another station in nine months." Joan Donkin remembers walking, cycling and swimming and "dear Mrs Mitchell" who lived near Landewednack church "who must have served hundreds of teas to us girls in her teeny-tiny sitting room. Her thinning hair was scraped back into a little bun on top of her head and she wore long black dresses, old-timey boots and starched white aprons. She seemed to have popped right out of the Victorian age. She was jolly and laughing......and made the most delicious Cornish pasties I have ever tasted. There would also be scones and jam and on occasion even a small dab of Cornish cream."

Joan enjoyed dancing and every so often they organised dances in the mess where Solly Solomon, a Canadian radar mechanic, showed his skill in jitterbugging. However Falmouth was the Mecca to make for when time allowed where the Services Club held "fantastic dances". But the trouble as usual in an isolated position was how to get there. The only bus took two-and-a-half hours to travel the twelve miles from Helston to Falmouth, because of all the detours to include the villages. However she and her friends had become skilled hitchhikers and even riding in the back of a tiny Austin 7 truck with dead rabbits was worth it. More usually the friendly Americans, who were now appearing in great numbers with their military vehicles, supplied the necessary transport on many occasions.

The absence of much social life might have been responsible for a murder connected with the Pen Olver station and later ghostly sightings. The station commander, Flying Officer William Croft, had an affair with one of the young WAAF radar plotters, Corporal Joan Lewis, a lively dark-haired girl, billeted at the Housel Bay Hotel. This was against all protocol and was made worse by the fact that he was a married man with two children. When he was tackled about this by the officer in charge of the

Radar - the Secret Weapon

girls, he and Joan decided that she should apply for a transfer, which might not be too far away.

They had one last week-end together and then early on a cold October morning in 1943 two shots were fired in the summer house in the hotel garden. The first that anyone else knew about the tragedy was when Croft admitted to her murder on the phone to another officer. When this was investigated the girl was found lying dead, shot in the chest and through the head. Croft later changed his story to a suicide pact which he could not complete. He was found guilty of murder, but his death sentence was later changed to life imprisonment.

At the time, the murder was hushed up as much as possible. Joan Donkin, who was posted there about two months later, found that the summer house was boarded up and out of bounds and "no one wanted to talk about it." Later, stories began to circulate of a ghost in the garden dressed in WAAF uniform, to be seen only in October, and on one such occasion she was sketched by an artist who was staying at the hotel more than thirty years later.

The build-up of American forces, which Joan noticed during the early months of 1944, was heralding the approach of D-Day.* She and her colleagues saw the increase in shipping around the coasts, knew that their letters were being censored and civilian movement severely restricted and then all leave was cancelled. "I remember well on D-Day sitting in the mess and listening to a recorded message from General Eisenhower that the invasion had indeed started." What she probably did not realise was the important part that radar played in the success of this momentous operation.

D-Day could stand for Deception Day, because so much effort was put into confusing and misleading the German authorities, and radar played a vital role in this charade. In the months leading up to June, bombers equipped with high-powered jamming equipment began to patrol the south coasts to produce a "curtain" behind which, unseen by the German radar operators, the shipping build-up could increase. German radar stations were bombed and careful note was taken of how long it was before they were back in operation. Dummy convoys sailed out and small boats equipped with large radar-reflecting balloons floating above them moved through the Channel. These were escorted by the Dambuster Squadron which dropped "window", silver foil strips which jammed radar while it fell through the air, making it look as if an invasion fleet was on its way. Then one month before D-Day, secret Mandrel transmitters were switched on to create a curtain of remote "white noise" close to the English coast. Slowly the intensity was increased as the curtain was projected closer and closer to the French coast.

Radar - the Secret Weapon

The Allied military authorities must have been particularly worried that in spite of all these careful preparations there was a bad air raid on Falmouth,* one of the embarkation ports, only a week before D-Day, when sailors and troops were massed in the area ready to start loading the following day. People were killed and much-needed fuel was lost when a petrol storage tank had a direct hit, but the secrets of the invasion still remained intact.

By D-Day 200 vessels were equipped with Mandrel transmitters and when the invasion fleet put to sea and the sealed orders were opened the first instruction was to switch these on. The white noise and the less than favourable weather conditions made life for the German radar operators tiring and uncomfortable. The invasion fleet was so effectively hidden that the German defences in Normandy were taken by surprise and the landing on the beaches proved successful.*

The war was now moving away from the shores of Britain and radar coverage was gradually reduced. Treleaver continued for a time for the use of Fighter Command but then like many other sites, it stopped operating and was put on a care and maintenance basis in April 1946. To many people war is about fighting men and their exploits. They forget that success in the field is often the result of hard work behind the scenes by a very large number of people. The work of the radar scientists, operators and mechanics had to be kept secret during these years, when victorious battles were being trumpeted by the media. By the time details of their work could be made known the war was over and many people wanted to forget this time of death, destruction and privation and look forward to the future. So the work of these people was sometimes overlooked.

However the strategic position of the Lizard area was not forgotten. The cold war with Communist Russia dominated foreign politics after 1945, and in November 1947 reports came through that Russia had exploded her first atomic bomb at a secret site in Siberia. Radar was seen once more as an important part of the country's defence system. In the early 1950s a huge radar bunker was built at Treleaver to act as an early warning system, until it was superseded by the station at Fylingdales in Yorkshire.

A decade later, on 11 July 1962, the Goonhilly Satellite Earth Station received the first live transatlantic television broadcast from Telstar, showing the importance for communications of this isolated site today.

Postscript One of the most important radar inventions was the cavity magnetron, which worked on a very short wavelength and gave the Allies a commanding lead in radar technology during the war. When Henry Tizard led a mission to Canada and the USA in 1940, he carried one of these with him to show that Britain was still in a position to fight back

Radar - the Secret Weapon

against Germany. As a result he secured the vital supplies that Britain needed and Canada's participation in research and development. An example of this highly sensitive and secret equipment, which one guarded with one's life at the time, was recently found in a car boot sale in Cornwall and bought for £3.

From radar bunker to bungalow, Trelanvean. (V. Acton)

7. "THE EYES AND EARS OF ALL OUR DEFENCES"

Young Dunstan Thomas pedalled up the hill through the dark tunnel of trees. It felt eerie in the stillness and blackness of the night, but he had a job to do and it was an important one. He had been accepted into the Royal Observer Corps, young though he was, because he had impressed Mr Splatt, the butcher, with his ability to recognise the different types of aeroplanes. Mr Splatt had showed him cards, when he had come to Dunstan's home on his delivery rounds, on which were printed the black silhouettes of aircraft and the teenager had reeled off the names, British and American as well as German. This was an ability that the Observer Corps needed and so he was soon regularly cycling up to the Penventon Observer Post, overlooking Helston, to do his stint of duty.

This post, like the other thirty-six posts in Cornwall, had a fine field of vision. From it observers could see the tall masts of the radar station at Dry Tree and from it too they saw the fearful orange glow in the sky as Plymouth burned, and the flashes on the horizon when Allied bombers were busy over Brest. Ever since the autumn of 1940 men had been watching from this post, reporting to Truro on enemy activity over their part of the Cornish coast.

The Royal Observer Corps had its origins in the South-East when bombs were dropped on London, without any prior warning, by German Zeppelin airships during the First World War. It was officially formed in 1924 and spread rapidly in the 1930s as the threat of war increased, but Cornwall remained outside this defence curtain until after the start of the Second World War. On 26 August 1940 Number 20 Group was formed with its headquarters in Truro in the GPO Exchange, with a direct link to Number 10 Fighter Group based at Box in Wiltshire. Its primary function was to provide an overland air-intelligence network for the RAF.

During that year twenty-six Observer Posts were hurriedly set up all round the county, from Saltash in the east to Sennen in the west, from Newquay on the north coast to Veryan on the south, and down the spine of the county from Callington to St Breward, Bodmin and Penryn/Stithians. Helston's post opened in October along with eight others. The need for them became imperative as bombing raids had begun on Cornish ports and military sites. This was the time of fear - the fear of a German invasion.

"The Eyes and Ears of All Our Defences"

All these posts were situated on high ground, mostly near the coast, where visibility was good. Telephone lines were quickly laid to link them with the group centre at Truro, and some were also linked to coastguard look-outs. Helston was linked to two, at Coverack and Porthleven. If enemy ships were seen approaching the shore, the coastguards were to report immediately to the coastal observer post to which they were connected. From there the information was passed by the centres to the RAF fighter sectors and on to the military authorities. If airborne landings were made the corps, perhaps informed by the Home Guard, would pass on the details in the same way.

If communication with the centre broke down, the posts were supplied with red-star rocket flares, which were to be fired in the event of a landing by enemy parachutists. If, because of invasion, the post had to be evacuated, then telephone lines were to be cut and all instruments taken away or destroyed. In this way the Observer Corps played a key role in the invasion-warning system.

Thankfully no invasion was made, but over the course of the next few years the corps made a vital contribution, not only in passing on intelligence about enemy aircraft, but reporting on many other activities such as surface craft, submarines, mine laying, aircraft or shipping in distress, rescues at sea, explosions, drifting barrage balloons and suspicious persons. One other very important task they did was to help friendly, lost aircraft return to base safely.

It had been assumed that radios would help lost aircraft return, but these could be damaged in fighting or be affected by electrical storms. A pilot was then left in limbo with no lights to guide him overland in blacked-out Britain. He might fly until he ran out of fuel and then crash, killing himself and his crew, and destroying a much needed plane. Some observer posts, such as St Ives, Nanpean and Helston, were equipped with HSL, homing searchlights, for directing fighters to the nearest airfield, but these could draw unwanted attention to their positions if enemy aircraft were around. Airfields began to install high-frequency short-range radio sets with a useful range of ten miles. These "Darky" sets, as they were code-named, were later extended to some of the observer posts, such as at Polperro, Veryan and Sennen. It has been estimated that in the country as a whole more than seven thousand lost or damaged aircraft were saved because of the Observer Corps.

These observer posts were small, equipped with a table having a large map of the area divided up into squares, and a vertical height scale, for estimating the position of aircraft. The observers became expert at working out the height of planes from studying the contrail, the condensed vapour trail, of planes flying high at twenty thousand to thirty thousand feet, the

"The Eyes and Ears of All Our Defences"

height varying according to temperature, being lower in winter. In foggy conditions they had only the sound of the aircraft to give them clues. No wonder that Herbert Morrison, the Home Secretary, described the Corps as the "eyes and ears of all our defences."

Information on the number, height and direction of planes was passed on to the centre at Truro, which could then confirm these details, with the information passed on by the neighbouring observer positions. Helston was code-named Q2, with Q3, the Lizard, to the south of them and Q1, Black Rock, to the north near Camborne.

They worked around the clock on shifts, two at a time, but with the change-over staggered every four hours to give continuity. Some worked full-time, a forty-eight hour week for 1s.3d an hour, although a teenager, like Dunstan Thomas, only received 9d an hour for a thirty-nine hour week when he joined in 1943. They usually did eight-hour shifts, while the part-timers did four hours.

Conditions at Penventon were not exactly comfortable. The hut was about seven or eight feet square, with one chair in a small cubby hole and, until hinged windows were fitted on the windward side, it could be very cold and exposed, which made the heavy overcoat supplied to them a vital necessity. Welcome cups of tea could be brewed in a small hut nearby equipped with a primus stove.

One perennial problem for the corps was the continual disappearance of the younger members as they were called up into the services at the age of eighteen. So in July 1941 women were admitted into this male organisation. Without this feminine intake the whole organisation could have collapsed in the later stages of the war. This meant changes: limits on the dirty stories and swearing, and extra facilities provided if possible.

During 1942-3 changes were made to improve communications as German tactics changed. Early in 1942 low-level raids by German fighter-bombers began, roaring in at wave-top height to avoid radar detection. These tip-and-run raids were difficult to deal with and the visual sightings by observers could be the first warning. All the observer posts had to be checked to assess the visibility for these low flights. As a result some satellite posts were set up, such as at Coads Green, St Just-in-Penwith, and Pentargus Point near Veryan, each manned by a single observer.

In addition some of the posts were equipped with snowflake illuminating rockets, code-named "Totter", to give immediate warning to AA gun crews and patrolling fighters, of hostile aircraft below one thousand feet. Nine Cornish posts were given these in 1942, including Helston, Par and Mevagissey, and seven more were installed the following year, including St Agnes, St Anthony and St Columb Major.

"The Eyes and Ears of All Our Defences"

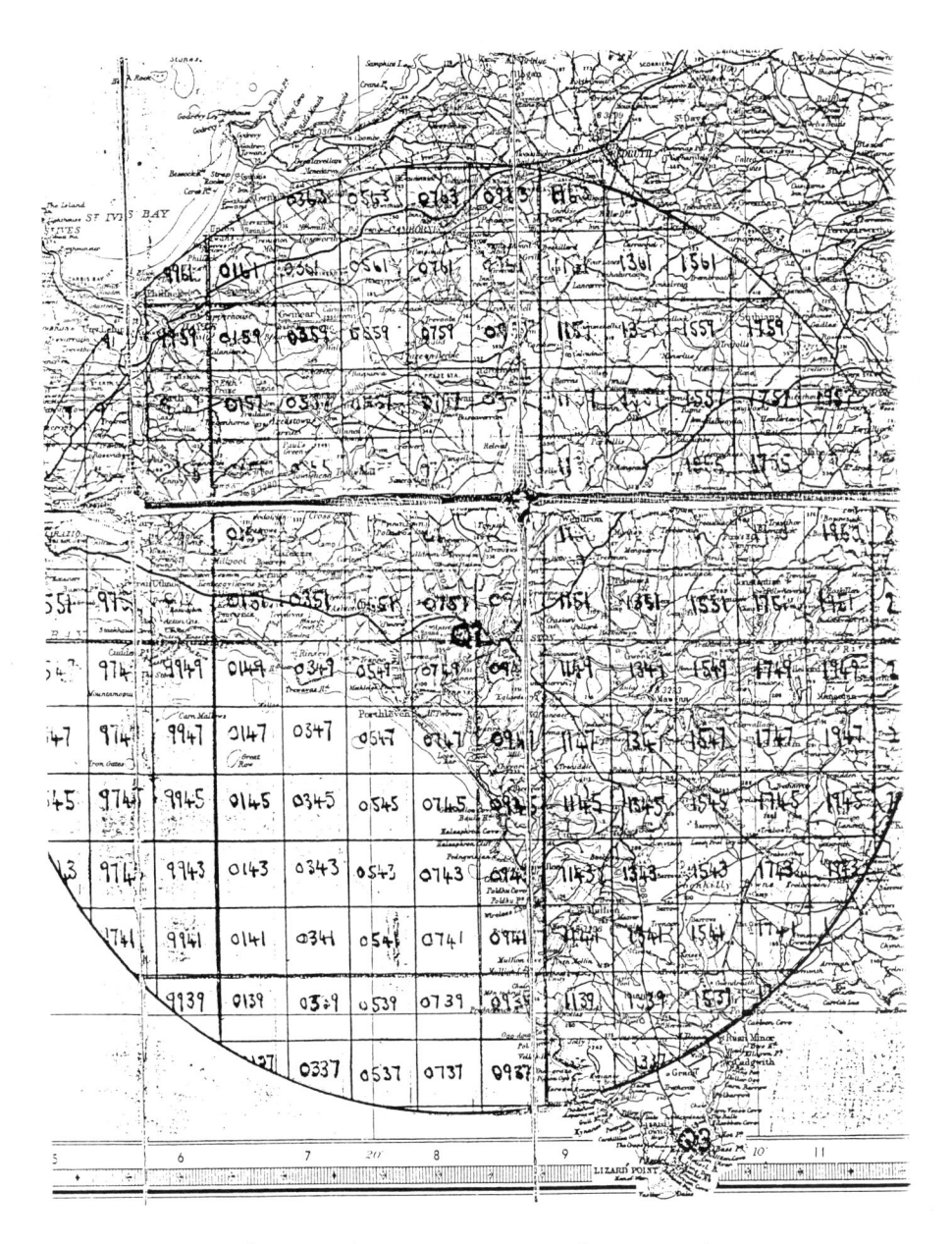

Squared map used at Q2, Penventon, Helston. *(D. Thomas)*

"The Eyes and Ears of All Our Defences"

During 1942 heavy raids were made on historic towns, such as Exeter, where on the night of 3/4 May, high explosive and incendiary bombs wiped out much of the centre of the city, and the ROC group centre was set on fire. Truro also suffered a bad raid later in August of that year, but on a much smaller scale, when the hospital was hit and people killed.*

The group centre here was moved from the GPO Exchange to the Masonic Hall in Union Place and was set out in a new way known as the "inland reporting system". In this, officials such as the controller and teller, were seated on a balcony overlooking the main map-table where the plotters were working. A new feature was a long-range map, manned by nine observers, positioned vertically where it could be easily seen by both the people on the balcony as well as the plotters at the main table. With this equipment, approaching raids could be detected in advance and with Cabinet approval in June 1943, group centres had a new official whose job was to activate the air-raid alarms for the town. The first of these "standard" centres to be ready was Truro's at the end of that month.

Truro's centre was now linked to the radar station at Treleaver on the Lizard, where the GCI (Ground Control Interception) system was in operation. This could provide both interception control and surveillance and the ROC was used as a manual gap-filler. At Truro there was a GCI interrogator, and at Treleaver the new position of ROC agent.

One other change that was made at this time to increase the speed of communications was the code word "Rats". This was the new priority message for "low raid urgent" which took too long. Now "Rats" followed by the grid letter and number of the post, alerted the centre, which could then pass the message on rapidly to the military authorities. These destructive low-flying raids decreased towards the end of 1943 partly because they were becoming too costly for the Luftwaffe, as the improvements in the speed and efficiency of British communications proved their effectiveness.

By this time Cornwall was beginning to be "invaded", not by the enemy, but by friendly American airmen, GIs and sailors. The skies became busier with training flights and bombing sorties, with damaged planes being reported as they limped back to base from raids over France. The moors and shores saw increasing activity as tank units tried out their weapons and vehicles, landing craft were tested and infantry trained to advance under fire. These were the months leading up to D-Day 6 June 1944, and the invasion of Normandy.

At the end of April 1944 a request was made for ROC volunteers to join "forthcoming operations". Their observation skills were to be of vital importance during the crossing of the Channel to Normandy. As the communiqué said, "The highest importance is attached to this request, for

"The Eyes and Ears of All Our Defences"

ROC Helston. From L to R. Back: Broad, Coles, Ralph, Forrester, Thomas, Mitchell, James, Splatt. Front: Kingdom, Rickard, Greenwood (C/Obs), Pryor. *(D Thomas)*

"The Eyes and Ears of All Our Defences"

inefficient and faulty recognition has contributed largely to enemy successes against our shipping and to losses of aircraft from friendly fire. .....No other organisation possesses our skill and experience in aircraft recognition." (One person who had died earlier in the war, when her plane had possibly been shot down by accident over the Thames Estuary, was the air pioneer Amy Johnson, who had become famous for her solo flight from Britain to Australia in 1930.)

The ability of the ROC was now fully recognised. During these years they had organised aircraft recognition tests, for which proficiency badges were awarded to the successful members; but success to them meant 100%, nothing less would do. Dunstan Thomas remembers going to the Plaza Cinema in Truro when, under subdued lighting, the screen was filled with aircraft - all types, from all angles - and all had to be correctly recognised for that badge. He scored 98%, just two short of success. It was for ability like this that their role would be so important, as the huge armada of invasion craft crossed in the short summer night to France. The skies would be throbbing with aircraft and mistaken identity could be fatal.

Over one thousand observers reported to the depot at Bournemouth where they undertook tests, from which nearly eight hundred emerged as petty officers in the Royal Navy. By the middle of May many were being drafted to their ships and by D-Day, five hundred were on board to take part in the historic voyage. On that day observers, who were on duty at their posts in Cornwall, saw waves of aircraft passing over, the underside of their wings painted in broad bands of black and white with more stripes on the fuselage. This was the identification for D-Day.

After the struggle for the beaches and the battle for Normandy, the war was passing away from the shores of Britain. Air-Vice Marshal Ambler of Fighter Command said "The ROC is an integral part of the command and without it command becomes practically non-operational. The whole plotting and radar system is bound up with the ROC." Four days after VE Day the ROC was stood down.

Early on in the war Winston Churchill had described the organisation as "Stone Age", after he had witnessed the marvels of radar, but on 10 June 1945 when King George VI, Queen Elizabeth and Princess Elizabeth attended a farewell parade in Hyde park of 2,500 representatives of the "citizen armies of civil defence", pride of place in that parade was given to the Royal Observer Corps.

8. CORNISH AIRFIELDS

The first edition of the *Woman's Daily Newspaper* on 7 November 1938 carried this main headline: *Call for Complete Abolition of Aeroplanes*. It then went on to say:

"There is only one way to deal with the aeroplane menace. That is the complete and absolute abolition throughout the world of all forms of air transport. The aeroplane has brought nothing but misery in its train. Quite apart from the hundreds who have lost their lives in ordinary accidents it is the aeroplane which has put the edge on war and made it the horror it is today."

The film footage of German air attacks on Spanish towns in the civil war there had had their effect. But there was no going back on technological advances.

With the fall of France in June 1940 Cornwall came close to the front line of the war. The number of operational airfields soon increased from the one, at St Eval, to eight, mainly down the northern side of the county, from Cleave near Bude, to Predannack on the Lizard. Over the next months and years the skies became increasingly noisy with aircraft intent on their varied tasks including bombing raids, fighter escort for bombing missions and secret operations across the Channel, U-boat detection and destruction, convoy escort and protection, photographic reconnaissance, air-sea rescue, ferrying aircraft to military operations overseas, and training. Airfields became ports of entry and exit for VIPs, both civilian and servicemen, and later American aircraft made their first landings in Cornwall from the long haul across the Atlantic.

From being an area regarded as of little strategic importance, Cornwall's position between the Channel and the Atlantic became vital. The highest operational airfield was on Davidstow Moor, the most southerly airfield was at Predannack on the Lizard and the most westerly was on St Mary's in the Isles of Scilly.

The speed with which many of these airfields were constructed shows how important they were thought to be. At Nancekuke, near Portreath, the farmers were expecting a good harvest in the summer of 1940, and food was usually given high priority. But before the crops could be gathered in, machinery was being driven ruthlessly through the fields, hedges were

Cornish Airfields

being levelled, houses knocked down with scant time for the occupiers to move out, and by March of the following year Spitfires and Hurricanes were flying into their new base at RAF Portreath. During the course of that year four more airfields became operational including two satellites for Portreath, at Perranporth and Predannack.

One of the main threats to the country was the attacks on merchant shipping bringing vital supplies to Britain. If the sea communications were severed then the country was doomed. The packs of U-boats lurking in the Atlantic, the fast E-boats hunting in the coastal waters as convoys arrived and departed and German fighter planes and bombers bringing danger from the skies, all had to be combated. The Allied planes based on the Cornish airfields played an important role in dealing with these threats.

The airfields, not surprisingly, came under attack themselves. William Joyce, or Lord Haw Haw as he was called, regularly broadcasting German propaganda, frequently mentioned St Eval as a prime target for German raids. In one bad raid the Naafi received a direct hit and during the early months of 1941 very few nights went by without an attack of some sort. The worst of these raids was when twenty-one people were killed from a direct hit on a shelter on January 25 1941.

St Merryn suffered from its share of air raids, in one of which ninety bombs were dropped on the camp. Judy McSwiney, who worked in communications there, remembers running for the shelter "watching with one eye a German Dornier coming in from the sunset to drop its load" and a sailor in her shelter broke his back from the power of the blast.

Soon after Portreath became operational, a series of raids was made, the worst being in May 1941 when forty high-explosive bombs were dropped, killing one airman, wounding three others and destroying or badly damaging six planes.

This month was a bad one for much of Cornwall, with fatal bombing raids in several places* including Falmouth, Penryn and Mawnan Smith and damage in many other areas. There was also a fatal attack on a convoy off the north coast, when one vessel, the *Mari-Flore*, was set on fire and forced to beach at Padstow, with six of the thirteen crew reported as missing. To try and counteract this threat, long-range Spitfires were brought in to both Portreath and Perranporth, which would have a greater chance of catching the bombers before they could return to the safety of their bases, and would also have some deterrent effect.

The German heavily-armed warships were adding to these dangers. The *Bismarck* was sunk in May 1941 but there were others that were taking their toll of Allied shipping. The *Gneisenau* had sunk or captured twenty-two vessels in one sortie lasting twenty days. In April 1941 she was in port at Brest when two Beauforts from St Eval went in to attack her. In

Cornish Airfields

Hurricane crew from 247 Squadron at Predannack, May 1941. *(P. West)*

Cornish Airfields

something like a suicide dive one of these, piloted by Flying Officer Kenneth Campbell, roared down to fifty feet before it released its torpedo. The plane was shot down and the crew were killed, but the *Gneisenau* was put out of action for eight months, severely damaged below the waterline. The twenty-three-year-old pilot was awarded a posthumous VC.

Three months later a larger-scale attempt was made on the warship, still in port at Brest, and now joined by the *Scharnhorst*. Operation Sunrise, as this was code-named, consisted of eighteen Hampden bombers escorted by seven fighter squadrons of Spitfires, all from the Portreath sector. They shot down four German fighters trying to penetrate their protective shield, a feat which earned the thanks of Air Vice Marshal "Bomber" Harris.

This was not the last Cornish attempt to destroy these great ships. A few days both before and after Christmas, sorties were made against Brest, with fighter escort provided by Predannack and Portreath. After the second of these the Portreath records state "6 Luftwaffe fighters shot down, 11 damaged." However, in spite of all these attacks the ships were not destroyed.

A blockade of the port of Brest was mounted to keep them bottled up out of harm's way, but on 12 February 1942, they slipped out into the Channel and escaped with the cruiser, *Prinz Eugen*, and five escort destroyers. This was a humiliating blow for the British, at a time when the news seemed particularly bad: Singapore fell to the Japanese forces three days later and the toll on merchant shipping in the Atlantic was rising alarmingly. Four days later eight Hurribombers of the Canadian Air Force (Hurricanes with bombs slung under each wing) flew into Perranporth to prepare for a revenge attack.

The five destroyers, which had escorted the German pocket battleships in their escape, were spotted returning towards the port of Brest. Six of these Hurribombers, escorted by Spitfires, now took them by surprise off the Breton coast, destroying one and severely damaging a second.

As the war progressed procedures were analysed for their effectiveness. Close attention was paid to the way radar was used, and collaboration between the RAF and scientists led to a new branch of science - Operational Research. 502 (Whitley) Squadron of Coastal Command at St Eval came under study for five months from the summer of 1942.

The regular patrols that were needed to protect the convoys meant that the planes required constant maintenance. But when it was realised that aircraft were flying on average only one sortie a week a team, led by Dr Cecil Gordon, was instructed to look into this and see if it could be improved, because there was a shortage of suitable planes to deal with the

U-boat menace. They found that it was usual for nearly one-third of all the aircraft to be grounded at any one time.

They studied the usual procedures and then assessed whether pilots could increase their flying hours without the onset of operational fatigue and whether the maintenance organisation could cope with this increase. They gradually increased the flying by one sortie a day, whenever the weather was suitable, until there was always one aircraft awaiting manpower. As a result it was decided that increasing the efficiency of maintenance was the answer.

The experiment was very successful and the squadron exceeded its own maximum flying effort per aircraft by sixty-one per cent, and also exceeded the best average of any squadron over a single period by seventy-nine per cent. As a result a system of planned flying and maintenance was devised for the whole of Coastal Command, and eventually throughout the RAF.

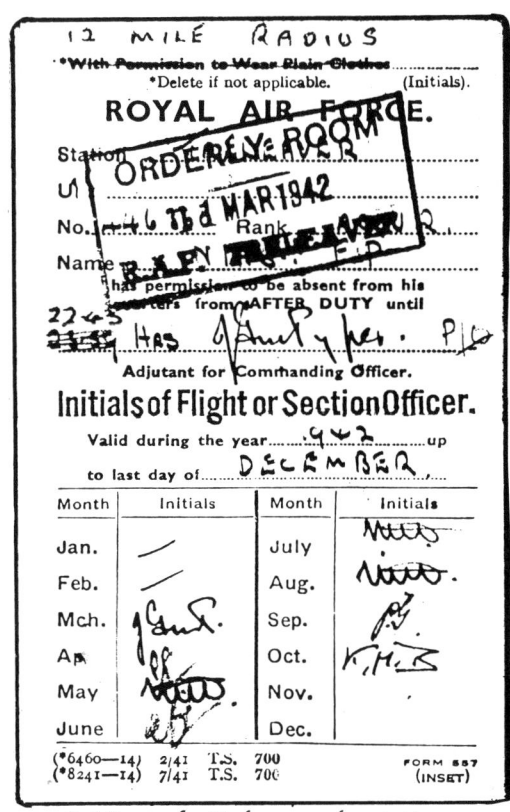

RAF pass for Treleaver radar station.

Cornish Airfields

The development of radar increased the effectiveness of air power, with better communications from the ground and greater accuracy in pinpointing targets. Records at Predannack emphasise the "splendid work by the GCI unit at Treleaver", which made possible the destroying of a Heinkel early in January 1942.

Six months later, Margaret Diplock, one of the radar plotters there, remembers being on duty one evening when there was another successful kill. A Beaufighter, Mullet 32, from Predannack was on convoy-escort duty off the north coast on the evening of 7 June. The pilot was a Cornishman, Albert Harvey, who had been born in Coverack and had a tobacconist shop in Falmouth. He and his observer, Bernard Wicksteed, were directed to intercept a German plane, which they spotted flying so close to the water that its slipstream was sending up spray from the sea. The records at Portreath explain what happened next.

"Plt Off Harvey attacked and, in spite of the fact that his starboard engine was set on fire, pressed home his attack and set fire to the port engine of the Heinkel III, which was later confirmed as destroyed. The Beaufighter also crashed into the sea. Plt Off Harvey assisted his observer onto his own dinghy, which by swimming, he pushed towards the coast, 7 miles away, for an hour. He then became exhausted and climbed onto the dinghy himself. After being afloat for 5 hours and when approx 200 yards from the shore, he swam ashore, scaled a cliff in pitch blackness, walked to the Ops room and organised a search party for his observer."

The airman on guard at the Operations Room at Tehidy Barton is reported as saying "Please Sir, a dripping Mullet 32 is at the door. Shall I let him in?"

Both Harvey and Wicksteed were awarded medals for their action. It was later confirmed that the Heinkel was in fact a Junkers 88 D5, which belonged to the German Long-range Reconnaissance Group.

The Operations Room for Portreath became the main control centre for mid and west Cornwall. When it first opened, temporary accommodation above a bakery on the Portreath road just outside Redruth was used. Here in the upstairs room was a plotting table and sets of telephones. Later, at the end of May 1941, the move was made to Tehidy Barton, about two miles from RAF Portreath, and this became the Sector Operations Room. Here radar stations, including those on the Lizard, sent in reports on enemy movements and from here the fighters were scrambled to intercept hostile planes.

Cornish Airfields

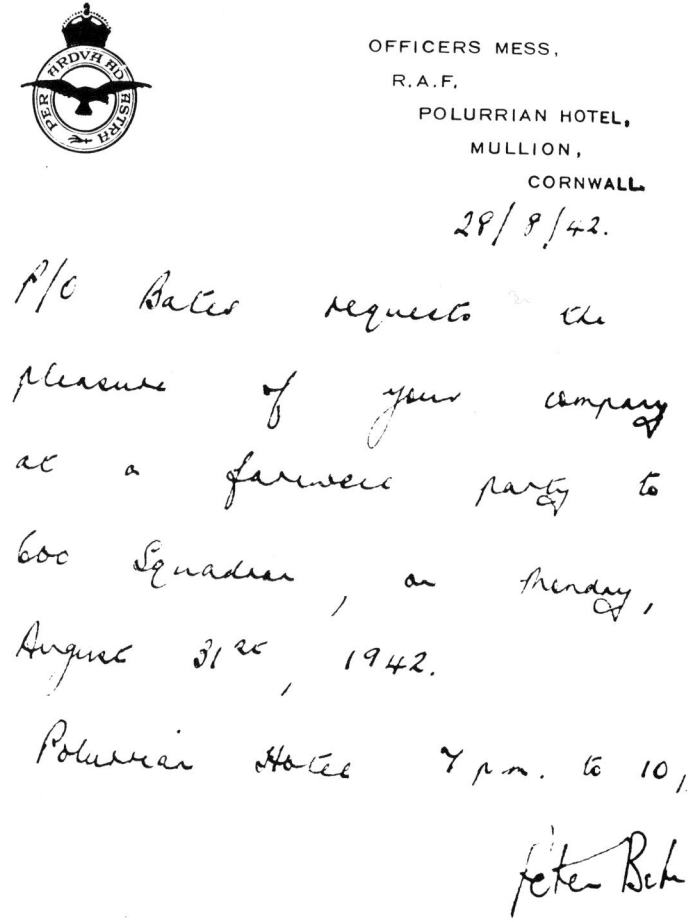

OFFICERS MESS,
R.A.F.
POLURRIAN HOTEL,
MULLION,
CORNWALL

29/8/42.

P/O Bates requests the pleasure of your company at a farewell party to 600 Squadron, on Monday, August 31st, 1942. Polurrian Hotel 7 p.m. to 10.

Peter Bch

Invitation to the farewell party for 600 Squadron at Predannack, August 1942.

Just over two years later the last move was made, to the Gin Palace as it was soon nicknamed; a purpose-built concrete bunker with more spacious accommodation and up-to-date equipment, situated on Tregea Hill overlooking Portreath. After the war this building became a pub with windows made to give wide views over the cliffs and sea, so the nickname proved very appropriate. However at the time there were no windows with panoramic views; entry was down steps from the higher level behind, and Peggy Riley (née Morris), who was a radar operator there, was convinced that the building was underground, until she returned for a reunion many years later.

Cornish Airfields

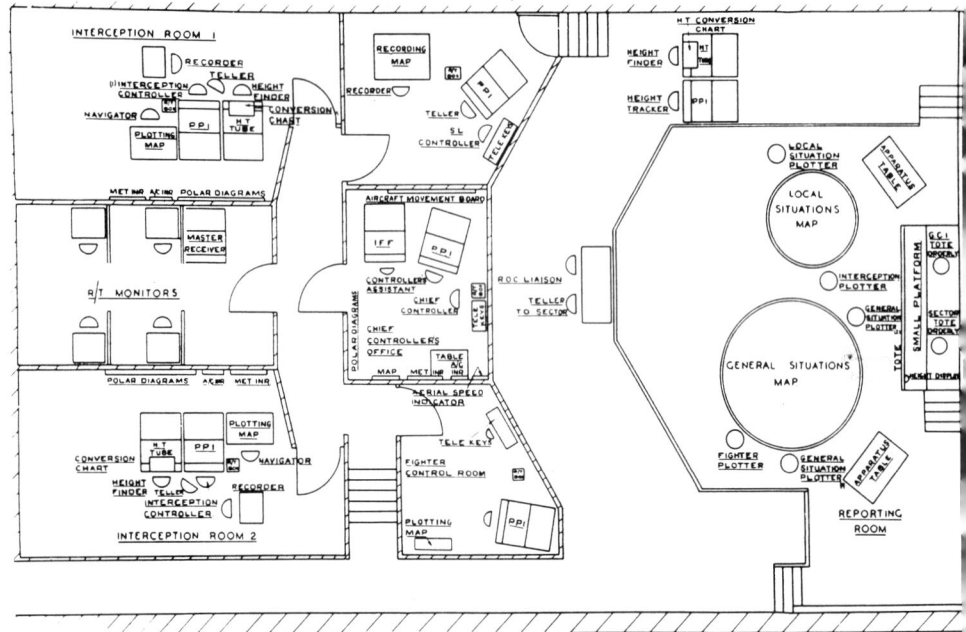

Typical Ops Room layout.

When the new control centre opened in July 1943 activity on the airfields was at an even higher level. This was a crucial stage of the war and Predannack was kept particularly busy that summer as a sample of the records show.

"1 June At 1105 hrs, a Beaufighter of 236 Sqn at Predannack, out on anti-submarine patrol, spotted U-418 in position 4705'N 0855'W. The Beaufighter at that time was carrying 8x25lb Rocket Projectiles (R/Ps). Fg Off Bateman (Pilot) fired off 2 pairs of R/Ps, and had to claim a seriously damaged hit."

(This was upgraded in September 1943 as a kill, as the R/Ps up until that date were secret, and intelligence did not want the kill to be placed on Official Records, because the type of weapon would also have to be recorded.)

Two days later another Beaufighter was set upon by eight Junkers 88s attacking in pairs. The pilot, Flight Lieutenant Shannon, dived to sea level to try and avoid them, but his Navigator was wounded and could not operate the rear guns. Shannon felt a bullet fly close by his head, which killed his Observer. The attack lasted for eight minutes during which time

Cornish Airfields

his plane suffered some extensive damage. But he managed to contact Predannack by radio and then limp back to the airfield for a belly landing.

June 14 was a particularly busy day for Mosquito Squadrons. In two separate actions they destroyed one German plane and damaged another, but that was not all. The day began with four Mosquitos from Polish and Canadian squadrons spotting a group of U-Boats, which they attacked in tight formation. They hit the conning towers on two of the boats, but in the strong defensive fire, the engine of one of the planes was damaged, and they then returned to Predannack. However they had the satisfaction of knowing that those two U-Boats were forced to return to their base at Lorient in Brittany.

In the afternoon four more were on patrol when they spotted four Junkers 88s, which they lost in the cloud cover. Only one of these four Mosquitos returned to base. The other three were last seen flying at sea level, but two messages were heard; one requesting an emergency homing to base and the other reporting that they were being chased by three FW 190s. After that there was nothing.

A few days later Mosquitos were again in action, attacking and destroying a German flying boat and then going on to the flying boat base at Biscarasse, where they attacked a hangar, hearing later that they had destroyed four of the planes. And so the operations continued.

Training was a vital part of the activities at many of the airfields. Peter Boving, a radar mechanic at Treleaver, recalls the daytime practices for the night fighter aircrews at Predannack, when they would beat in from the sea and shoot up the cliff and over the roof of the Headland Hotel at Coverack. He remembers that the local constable would moan about it because the noise upset the milk and egg production of his cows and hens.

Noise was also a problem for the people who lived at Factory Farm, close to the airfield at Portreath. Here planes would come in low and, just as they were flying over the farmhouse, they would start firing at the practice target set up on the edge of the airfield. Ernest Landry, who lived there then wrote, "The poultry round the farmyard used to fly in all directions, and the farm animals were terrified. They started the practice with a machine gun and went on to bigger guns, the empty brass shells dropping all over the place. We had several narrow escapes. .....How we used to long for a foggy day."

Training was important not only for the new pilots but also for more experienced ones using new equipment. Peter Boving remembers that at Predannack they tried out one of Winston Churchill's ideas using an American bomber to carry a ton of batteries and a searchlight on the nose. "In flight the bomber flew with a couple of Hurricanes, one at each wingtip, using GCI radar to get behind enemy planes. The light was used to blind

Cornish Airfields

the enemy pilot, and the wingmen would close in for the kill. We practised with these people a few times on clear nights, but the idea was too complicated and too dangerous and I never heard of it becoming operational."

Another light device was the Leigh Light, used to illuminate submarines at night so that aircraft could then attack. The Portreath records give an instance of their successful use in September 1943 when a detachment of Leigh Light Wellingtons picked up a U-Boat on the ASV (Air to Surface Vessel) radar. They switched off their lights, circled around and then switched them on again, picking out the boat, which immediately opened fire. Six depth charges sent it to the bottom with no survivors.

RNAS St Merryn was different from the other airfields in the county as it was used by the Fleet Air Arm, as an air gunnery training establishment, known as HMS Vulture. Here new crews could train and operational squadrons could have refresher courses. Judy McSwiney, one of the Wrens stationed there, was taken, unofficially, on a couple of "joyrides." She flew in a Fulmer, which dive-bombed Gull Rock off Trevose, firing its guns. "What a noise the armament made!" she recalls.

Training flights involving targets off Trevose Head, had been made here with Skuas early in 1941 to practise for an attack on the *Gneisenau* and *Scharnhorst* in port at Brest, but this had been aborted as the crews were too inexperienced for such a difficult attempt.

Wrens at St Merryn, HMS Vulture. (J. McSwiney)

Cornish Airfields

Training flights increased as American planes and crews moved into Cornwall in increasing numbers. On 1 November 1942 the Portreath records state "Lt Col Simenson USAAF arrived at station to assume command of American aircraft." This was the time of Operation Torch, when large numbers of planes were assembled at Portreath and Predannack to be sent out for the invasion of North Africa. Between 9th and 17th of that month, two hundred planes were dispatched.

The Police War Diaries record a growing number of accidents involving Americans. In the summer of 1943 two American soldiers stationed at St Eval were killed and a third was injured when they climbed the barbed wire fence surrounding the minefield at Mawgan Porth. In September one of their huge Flying Fortresses was forced to land at the civil airport at St Just, luckily not causing any damage, but towards the end of the year a Liberator crashed at St Mawgan, killing the crew of eleven. Two days before Christmas, a Dakota from St Mawgan, crashed into the summit of Brown Willy on Bodmin Moor killing all four of its occupants.

Predannack experienced the emergency landing of one of the Flying Fortresses in May 1943. This huge bomber had been involved in a raid over St Nazaire, but on the return journey a navigational error brought the plane over the Brest Peninsula, where it flew through heavy flak, being hit several times and catching on fire. Three of the crew bailed out, but Sergeant Maynard Smith, one of the gunners, grabbed a hand extinguisher and began to tackle the fire, which was so hot that it was beginning to melt some of the rear fuselage structure. He found the tail gunner lying wounded, so administered first aid before fighting the flames again.

By this time German planes were adding to the plight of the crippled bomber, and in between efforts to douse the fire he operated the waist guns to try and beat them off. The heat by this time was detonating spare ammunition stored in boxes, so Smith threw these out of the plane or away from the roaring flames. For ninety minutes he fought the fire, grabbing every extinguisher he could find and then using his heavy flying jacket.

Meanwhile the pilot, Lieutenant Lewis Johnson, was valiantly struggling to get his stricken plane back to England. As the coast came into view, Smith, who could see it through the gaping hole in the fuselage wall, began to throw out every loose object he could lay his hands on to lighten the load. They came in low over the Cornish coast, where the welcome runway of Predannack gave them a smooth landing.

Emergency medical treatment was given to them at the airfield, before they were taken to the Royal Infirmary in Truro. Smith was later awarded the Medal of Honour, the American equivalent to the VC.

St Mawgan became the main base in Cornwall from which Americans flew. It had three operational runways and acted as a staging post for

Cornish Airfields

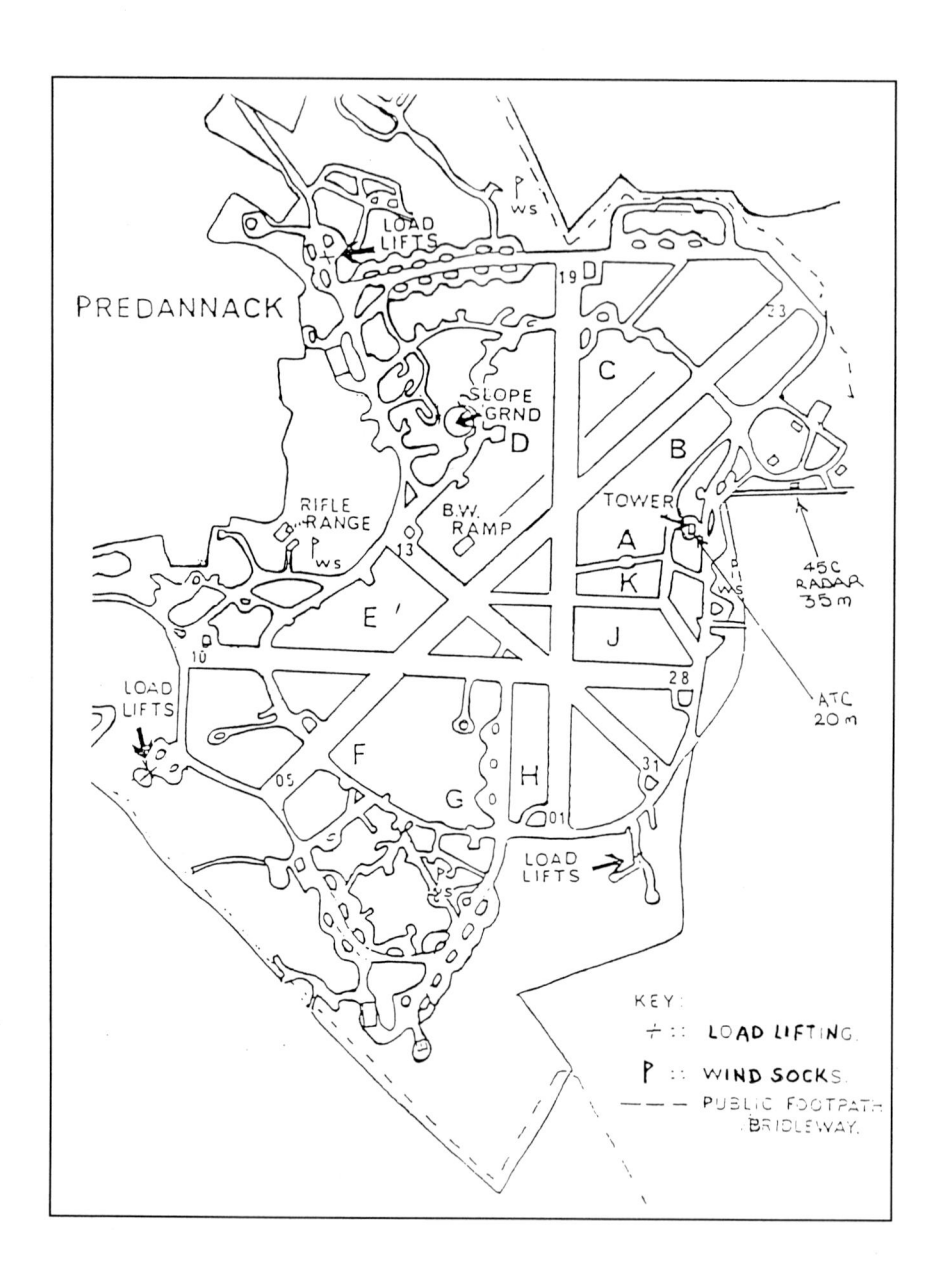

aircraft being sent out to North Africa, the Middle East and India. In the build-up to D-Day it became one of the busiest stations in the country handling over one hundred and fifty aircraft a day flying in from the States, sometimes desperate to land with fuel running low. Many of these planes were large, needing a long runway, which this airfield could provide by the middle of June 1943.

By the beginning of 1944 the tempo was quickening for the invasion of Normandy.* In January, General Eisenhower's deputy for D-Day, Air Chief Marshal Tedder flew into Portreath, escorted by a Free French Squadron. At Perranporth the briefing room became an operations centre for the Normandy invasions, Operation Overlord, and the nearby disused mine workings on Cligga Head were hastily converted into a bomb-storage area. Bombing raids over France, with attacks on French ports and shipping, built up. Then as D-Day, 6 June, dawned waves of planes filled the sky to bomb, carry paratroopers, act as a shield over the huge armada on the choppy seas below, and to patrol in carefully designated rectangular areas, or "corks", to attack any U-boats or other hostile shipping.

During the following months raids continued over France and then further east into Germany. By this time many planes became based in France and the activity on Cornish airfields gradually decreased. The war was not over by Christmas, as many had hoped, but the end was in sight and personnel began to leave the bases.

Wrens at St Merryn. Judy McSwiney front left in tricorn hat. (J. McSwiney)

Cornish Airfields

Hundreds of men and women had lived on these stations. Judy McSwiney writes of "a thousand men and about three hundred and eighty Wrens" at St Merryn. Portreath had over two thousand within a few months of opening and continued to grow, and at Predannack the numbers rose to about three thousand before D-Day. Most of these airfields were in isolated positions so leisure activities, very necessary to relieve tension, were limited.

At St Merryn, Judy McSwiney remembers that the Wrens there had only one weekend off a month and two weeks holiday a year, so there was not much time for pleasure-seeking. "Our entertainment was pretty simple by today's standards; with no cars and with very little money we were all in the same boat." She recalls the dances in the camp and in the village of St Merryn and the beautiful beaches nearby.

Netball teams: the Wrens of St Merryn v. the Waafs of St Eval. (J. McSwiney)

Her nineteenth birthday was made memorable when she was taken by three of her friends, one of whom had a car and using some illicit petrol they drove to the Victoria Inn at Roche. "There in front of a blazing fire, treat of all treats, we had eggs, bacon and champagne - unheard of luxuries."

She and her friend Audrey "had some marvellous evenings out, sometimes at the Trevose Golf Club. With the imposition of uniforms there was always the desire to innovate. Most of the pilots wore with their navy

Cornish Airfields

blue battledress, silk spotted scarves, very glamorous when their hats were squashed well down on their heads, completed by flying jackets and boots." She also adds, "Christmas was something I never enjoyed in the Navy. Most of the Ship's Company got very drunk and there seemed to be no other interest in the celebration."

The Personnel Booklet produced at Predannack starts with this paragraph.

"The common grouse of the newcomer to the camp is that Predannack is so far from everywhere; there are no large towns in the vicinity with the amenities and comforts of the modern world, and 'off-duty' hours cannot be quite as bright and cheerful as one might wish."

It then goes on to give details of what facilities were available both on the camp and nearby in Helston, from the Naafi and YMCA, to the music room and library, from the gymnasium and sports ground to the churches. The station cinema "is fitted with the latest up-to-date equipment ensuring perfect entertainment from the very best of recent films." Dances were organised twice a week for which airmen paid 3d, senior NCOs 6d, and officers and civilians 1s.

This airfield also had a "farm", where pigs were kept and some crops grown. Here airmen interested in post-war farming could be given instruction and were encouraged to join the Predannack Farmers' Union. During 1944 this scheme provided food to the value of £1,896.

When pig farming palled, the booklet assured all ranks that they could use their service bicycles for recreational purposes as well as service, but only within a ten mile radius. The wonderful

DO'S, DONT'S and OTHER THINGS.

Here, to conclude, are a few items of Camp Discipline and Routine that you should learn immediately, in case you find out by bitter experience.

(9) **Service Bicycles.** The privilege is granted to all ranks of using their service bicycles for recreational purposes as well as Service, governed by the following Bounds—the area bounded by a circle. the centre of which is R.A.F. Station Predannack and the radius 10 miles.

You Are Responsible For:

1. The safe custody of the bicycle. its tools and accessories, for which purpose users must supply their own locks and keys. or ensure that the bicycle, if left unattended, is in safe custody.

2. The replacement of all losses and items damaged by unfair wear and tear.

3. The care and repair of tyres and tubes.

4. Minor adjustments.

5. Reporting all damage or parts requiring replacements through fair wear and tear.

6. Keeping all parts clean and oiling where required:

7. Using it only for the purposes for which it is issued.

Cornish Airfields

facilities for bathing and swimming were mentioned with a warning about the strong and treacherous currents. For greater variety coaches could take personnel to Penzance, once a week for air crew and once a fortnight for ground crew.

With the end of the war in Europe approaching, arrangements were made to celebrate victory. On 4 May the Routine Orders gave the details, with this message from the Station Commander.

"Here are the arrangements made for VE Day and I want all personnel to attend these functions, including Officers.

"There will be an ALL Ranks Dance on the Station the evening of VE Day. All Officers and their wives, or lady friends are invited to attend. NCOs and Other Ranks may bring a civilian lady or male friend.

"Closing time will be governed by the behaviour of personnel. It is specially requested that no officer, NCO, or Other Rank over-celebrates as this will spoil the fun for all.

"The following morning starting at 10.30 hours there will be a Treasure Hunt on Bicycles, and I should like everyone to join in this. It would be possible to arrange this Treasure Hunt to include a few of the 'locals'.

"At 15.00 hours the same day a Sports Meeting will be held on the Station Sports Ground pitch, personnel may bring any civilian friends."

At Portreath the station closed down for forty-eight hours leaving on duty just the personnel needed for essential duties. It was recorded that "VE Day was something of an anti-climax, but special church parades were held in Camborne, Redruth and Truro with a strong RAF representation to express appreciation for the help and the warm hospitality they had received in this area."

Four months later Predannack and St Eval both welcomed in the public to celebrate Battle of Britain Day. The *West Briton* reports,

"Vehicles of all descriptions passed along the Helston-Lizard road to Predannack, and many pedestrians also made the journey, and all felt amply rewarded by the more intimate knowledge they gained of the great work of the RAF. .....As at Predannack so at St Eval, all members of the station laid themselves out to make the visitors feel at home. Over 1500 cars made the trip from near and far to St Eval, and 48 buses added their quotas to the crowds of visitors."

Cornish Airfields

In due course some of these airfields closed down, to revert to civilian use only, as in the case of St Mary's on the Isles of Scilly, or to return to farming. However the war had shown that Cornwall had strategic importance. The RAF kept a presence in the county at St Mawgan, and St Merryn was still being used in 1951: a *West Briton* report mentions that a Dutch Air Squadron was to be stationed there for some months. "It will be the first occasion in time of peace for Netherlands aviators to receive training on British soil." The main base for the RNAS in Cornwall was Culdrose, near Helston, HMS *Seahawk*. This had been developed during the war, but did not become operational until 1947. Its close neighbour, Predannack, closed in 1946 and later used for secret trials (Chapter 11), was also taken over by Culdrose.

The farmers at Nancekuke, who had been promised their land back after the war with compensation for damage, now found that not only was the airfield to stay in government hands but it was also to be enlarged. Factory Farm lost fifty-five acres, including much of its water supply, and sinister stories later began to circulate of strange goings-on behind its high perimeter fencing (Chapter 11). The war of six years had brought long-lasting changes.

9. VICTORY AND PEACE 1945

VICTORY IN EUROPE

From beaches and ports in Cornwall, American soldiers streamed across the Channel from 6 June and for many days after, as wave after wave of men were sent over for the invasion of Normandy.* One of these was Leigh Hooker of the 776th Anti-Aircraft Weapons Battalion.

This battalion had set up its guns on sites around the Fal and Helford rivers, with its headquarters at Trelissick House, near Feock. Leigh Hooker's gun, Yankee Wildcat, guarded the Helford, on the low headland close to the village near the ferry crossing. From there he saw the *Sunbeam* moored close by, saw the French fishing boats return from their secret operations, and heard the roar of powerful diesel engines when a boat left during the hours of darkness.

For a young man, far from home, who modestly describes himself as "never a good soldier", this time of waiting must have been difficult, but the friendship of local people helped. He still remembers with affection Mrs Winfrey, to whom the gun crew passed their rations, which she was then able to turn into seven-and-eight course meals for them. He recalls the exchange every Friday, of Lucky Strike cigarettes for Black and White Scotch Whisky, with Harold Roberts at the Shipwrights Arms, and then sitting on the patio looking down at the peaceful river while they all shared their "goodies." The people here helped him through what he describes as "a pretty hard time in my life."

Then as D-Day approached the alert went out to the gun crews, but for the 776th the orders were changed so that they could guard the loading hards, as the long lines of men and vehicles embarked for the Normandy beach, code-named Omaha. His gun was just up-river from one of these specially-made hards at Trebah, with its loading pier stretching out into the water. The battalion that replaced them for the initial invasion suffered badly, with three-quarters of its men casualties.

But their respite was not for long. He went across the Channel with the sixth wave of the invasion forces, aboard a "Rhino", a flat, square vessel. They landed on Omaha Beach and moved a short way inland to set up their gun at Insigny, a small port on the River Aure. Here he shot down his first enemy plane, a Junker 88. "My heart breaks even now when

Victory and Peace 1945

The point at Helford where "Yankee Wildcat" was based for a time in 1944. Leigh Hooker 2nd from right in picture below. (L. Hooker)

Victory and Peace 1945

I think of what a great pilot that German boy was." They were near the canal, which had concrete walls about twenty feet high. The pilot flew his plane in the dark along the canal just above the water and below the top of the walls. Leigh, an expert plane spotter, recognised it as an enemy plane, and "tracked him up and down the fuselage. It must have got the pilot because he stalled the plane - it sounded like someone shaking a bucket of bolts in a washtub, as he passed overhead. He went into a shallow glide and his right wing cut off a church steeple." (See Appendix 3.)

"Yankee Wildcat" pushing into Europe. Leigh Hooker leaning on tyre. (L. Hooker)

After the successful invasion of Normandy that summer, it had been hoped that the war would be over by Christmas. This was not to be. The campaign in Normandy took longer than expected, and then the Allied troops had to advance over a widening front, gradually pushing back the German forces: Paris was liberated on 25 August; Brussels on 4 September; Nancy, Hitler's key bastion in eastern France, on 15 September. There was then the failure of the Allied mission to capture the bridge over the Rhine at Arnhem, which if successful could have shortened the war by some months. But the first German city, Aachen, was captured on 20 October, and a month later American troops were in the vital German mining area of the Saar, British troops were advancing around Cologne and French troops were pushing into Germany from Strasbourg.

Victory and Peace 1945

But a week before Christmas, the Germans took the Allies completely by surprise, pushing westwards into Belgium through the lightly defended hills of the Ardennes, exactly the same area as their successful blitzkrieg advance in 1940. They advanced sixty miles into the Allied lines, through snowstorms and drifts, but as the weather cleared at the end of the month, the Allied bombers went into action and this Battle of the Bulge lasted well into January.

On 1 January 1945 the *West Briton* reported on "the bright, seasonable weather which is rare in Cornwall" and commented on the "freedom for the first Christmas in six years, from the menace of attack. ..... and above all, the rolling back from these shores of the tide of battle."

The tide of battle had not completely rolled back, however, for people living in the east of the country, as the fear of rocket attacks, which had begun soon after D-Day, still threatened those areas. The sudden silence in the buzz of a doodlebug, the VI, could announce to anxious listeners further death and destruction and even worse was the completely silent approach of the V2 rockets. The most deadly of these attacks was on 25 November 1944, when a V2 rocket hit a crowded Woolworth's store in south London, killing 168 and seriously injuring a further 108 people. People in Cornwall would have known few details on this and other attacks as strict censorship was imposed, but pleas went out to people here to give up their air raid shelters. These attacks continued until March 1945, but by this time headlines in the *West Briton* were indicating the final stages of the war in Europe.

29 January *Russians Drive Deep into Europe.*
15 February *Battle of Germany. 6,000 Allied Planes in Terrific Assault.*
26 March *In Steady Rain British Troops Battling Forward in Germany.*
23 April *Red Shock Troops Fighting for Berlin's Key Points.*
3 May *Nearing the End. Germany out of Italian Campaign. Berlin Captured.*
Before the next edition was published war in Europe was over, and the paper's headlines on 10 May were:
Days of Thanksgiving and Rejoicing. Cornwall Celebrates Victory in Europe. Truro Cathedral Filled to Overflowing.

The victory celebrations began on the evening of 7 May when: "at 10.30 bomb-scarred Falmouth resounded with the sirens and hooters of ships in the harbour and rockets, Very lights, searchlights and star shells illuminated the port and were visible for miles inland." This emphasis on blazing lights was a natural reaction to years of blackout. The government had allowed the restrictions on lighting to be partly lifted for two days, although because of fuel shortages full street lighting was still not allowed.

Victory and Peace 1945

Dutch cadets, who had been stationed at Enys near Penryn, line up for the Victory Parade, Falmouth. (RCPS)

As for Truro, the paper reports for the following day, "When evening fell Truro banished the darkness with hundreds of lights shining from houses, streets and gardens. Bonfires were lit, curtains were pulled back and the gas street lamps sprang alight for the first time for nearly six years."

For two days there was light, colour and noise as fires flamed, flags and bunting fluttered, bells rang, bands played and choirs sang in towns and villages all over the county. At St Day, Leonard Andrew remembers that fireworks were created by canon shells and other ammunition found on American dumps. Perhaps they had achieved some sort of expertise in this dangerous practice, as schoolboys sometimes threw bullets into the schoolroom fires for the excitement of it. In Grampound, described as "one of the best decorated villages", a huge bonfire was built and an effigy of Hitler burned, and this was repeated in other places.

Twice during the day on Tuesday 8 May there was a hush in the festivities as people gathered once more around their wireless sets, as they had done so often during the days of war. Now it was to hear first of all the voice of Winston Churchill giving the official announcement of the end of hostilities in Europe, ending with the words, "Advance Britannia. Long live the cause of freedom. God save the King." Later in the evening King George VI's more gentle voice was heard speaking from "our Empire's

The full official plans

By Daily Mail Political Correspondent

NEWS that the war in Europe is over will be given by the Prime Minister in a special B.B.C. broadcast This may be given by Mr. Churchill at any hour of the day or night in the very near future.

It will be followed by a broadcast by the King to the Empire, which has been fixed for nine o'clock on the night of VE-Day.

The day following, as well as VE-Day, will be a Public Holiday.

oldest capital city, war-battered but never for one moment daunted or dismayed."

Many places celebrated by dancing. In Bodmin crowds poured into Mount Folly Square and then danced up and down Fore Street. But it was not just the modern dances of the day, but in truly Cornish style the Flora Dance was seen winding its joyous way through streets in Lostwithiel, Tregony and Truro. People danced from the football ground in Treyew Road down the hill into the heart of the city and at the Royal Cornwall Infirmary "a drum was heard and a dance band emerged from a ward into the rose garden playing the haunting strains of the Cornish Flora Dance. It was followed by a long procession of gay and smiling nurses, dancing in great style to the music of the saxophone, drum and accordion." Marjory Jones (née Rule) was one of the nurses and writes of "the burning, blood-singing notes of the Floral dance.....the old, wild dance of victory."

VE Day happened to coincide with Helston's Furry Day, which had not been celebrated for most of the war years. Now arrangements were hurriedly made so that tradition and victory could be celebrated together. *"Helston Thronged for Festival"*, headlined the *West Briton*, which it went on to describe as "among the most successful in the long history of the ancient festival. ......From an early hour people began to pour into the town, and at about midday the crowd in the main thoroughfare to watch the children's dance was so dense that all traffic was held up."

The town was decorated for the occasion, not with the traditional green foliage, but with red, white and blue bunting. The only official dance was the children's, with so many men still away in the forces, and the sun smiled on the girls in their coloured dresses with flower garlands in their hair and the boys in white shirts with sprays of lily-of-the-valley. The Town Band, augmented by others, played their hearts out, not only for this dance but also for the two unofficial dances during the day.

Victory and Peace 1945

Flora Day & VE Day in Helston. 8 May 1945
Dancers include Rosemary Cowls, Porthleven, with Courtney Rowe, Kuggar; Susanne Eva, Manaccan with George Middleton, an evacuee in Manaccan; Jean Morrish, St Keverne; Sheila Clarke, St Keverne, with Olive Hall, Porthleven. *(S. Carter)*

The weather was certainly on the side of the revellers as temperatures soared in the afternoon to over 80 degrees in southern England. The following day national newspapers were allowed to give a weather forecast for the first time since 1 September 1939.

Many services were also held during these two days but the main thanksgiving services took place on the following Sunday, when churches were overflowing. Long parades led by bands marched through town and village streets, made up of not only members of the forces but also all those civilian organisations that had helped in the survival of the country, including the Home Guard, the Coastguards, the Police, The Royal Observer Corps, the Red Cross, the Women's Land Army, the Women's Voluntary Service, the British Legion and not forgetting the National Savings Committee workers, the Girl Guides and the Boy Scouts.

Over one thousand of these people packed into Truro Cathedral to hear Bishop Hunkin give thanks to all for their steadfastness and for "the deliverance of mankind from the menace and evil of Nazism." Foremost in many people's minds must have been the horror stories recently read in the national papers, as Allied troops liberated the concentration camps, although as the *Daily Mail* reported on 19 April, "much cannot be printed."

Victory and Peace 1945

Some of the men who saw the conditions there were troubled by nightmares for years after.

After this service the Mayor of Truro, Mr F Truscott, addressed the parade outside the Town Hall, thanking all, including "some who would be returning to their homes in the Dominions and the USA and he hoped they would carry away happy memories of their sojourn in this country." He also made a point of mentioning other homecomers, the returned prisoners of war to whom he offered "heartiest congratulations."

The *West Briton* had been reporting on a number of these reunions. On 26 April headlines read: *Captives Home. Released Prisoners Arrive in Cornwall.* The following article continued: "The past week has brought joy to many Cornish homes in the arrival of prisoners of war, or the news of their safe return to the country. Some have undergone considerable hardships during captivity." One Redruth man, who had been captured in North Africa, described his life in a German working camp as a "living hell", and he and many others praised the work of the Red Cross with their essential food parcels.

One Penryn woman, who six months earlier had been informed of the death of her grandson whom she had brought up, was amazed and delighted to hear that he was alive and just released from a prisoner-of-war-camp in Germany. The *West Briton* describes the home-coming of another Penryn man. "There was much jollification at the western end of the town when Sapper Sidney Rundle arrived at his home, 23 Glen View. He was a POW for nearly three years. A large banner hung across the road bearing the words 'Welcome Home'. Other similar messages were chalked on the gate of his house. The Mayor, Alderman H. Jennings, gave him a

LET the BELLS RING

but...

Let the bells ring for the half is done!
But after the bells a task remains.
The roof is safe, the fireside smiles,
but sons are away from their homes,
away ten thousand miles;
Burma, Borneo, Hong Kong, Singapore
Though half is done still half remains.
While they still fight shall we forget—
with a world to mend and wounds to heal?
The bells that ring to bid us rejoice
they also ring with a graver voice:
a sterner summons no man may shirk
to new beginnings and nobler work.

THANKSGIVING WEEKS

Victory and Peace 1945

hearty handshake." At Tregony on VE Day "Mr Henry Northcott, a prisoner of war, was greeted home by practically the whole village, decorated lorries and bands escorting him to his home, which was gaily decorated by neighbours."

For these people and many like them these days must have been ones of great relief and happiness, but for others the festivities would have seemed bitter-sweet. Many people must have been thinking of those who would never return, those killed by this terrible war. Even in the *West Briton* of 10 May, which was describing all the celebrations, there were photos of four local men who had been killed in action, two from Penryn, one from Goonhavern and one from Falmouth. Four days after these rejoicings one of the MGBs of the 15th Flotilla, MGB 2002, used in the secret operations across the Channel, was blown up by a floating mine and only two of the twenty-nine men on board survived. The war was not over and many homes must have been missing a son, father, husband or brother who was far away in Asia or who was soon to be on his way there. The *Daily Mail* of 19 April had carried a short article about pleas for the government to delay any organised victory celebrations until Japan was beaten, but these were not followed.

The newspapers of 8 May wrote about demobilisation for troops within six weeks, but they also included the less welcome news that young men who had been employed in industry would now be called up for military service. There was to be another three months of war before peace was finally declared.

In this uneasy interlude people tried to adjust to their new situation. At the end of May the Cornish Civil Defence forces were stood down. In July the Feock Women's Institute said goodbye to Channel Islanders who had been staying there, and who at long last could return to their newly-liberated islands. The Truro engineering company of HTP, which had done much essential war work, repairing Spitfire fighters in their car show rooms in Truro, now began to look to the future and in August obtained the first post-war car, an Austin. Visicks engineering works at Devoran, that had geared itself to supply war needs, now began to advertise its expertise for peace work; grinding and building up of crankshafts, valve reconditioning and metal spraying.

For the politicians the summer was the time of reckoning. During the war years there had been no general election, and all the parties had worked together under Churchill's leadership. Now party politics came to the fore again and election campaigns were fought all over the country, with the newest of the parties, Labour, striving for its first overall majority on 5 July with its manifesto, "Let Us Face the Future". The results were delayed until 26 July, to allow the service votes to come in from Germany,

Victory and Peace 1945

India and the Far East, and it was largely because of these that the second edition of the *West Briton* on that day was able to declare, *Big Swing to the Left Throughout Country. Labour Government with a Clear Majority. Penryn/Falmouth Returns the First Cornish Labour Member.*

This constituency had come close to electing a Labour member in the previous election in 1935, when A L Rowse, the historian, had forced the Liberals into third place and had polled only 3,000 fewer votes than the Conservative, Maurice Petherick, who had then remained the member for the whole of the war. Now this constituency was the one to best reflect the national trend. No other Labour MP was returned for Cornwall, but all three Plymouth seats became Labour controlled. The unthinkable had happened and Winston Churchill, who had led the country through its darkest days to almost the final victory, was no longer the leader.

The *Daily Mail* carried as one of its front page headlines the following day, *World is Stunned by Vote*. It then goes on to report "the most astonished of all countries was the United States;" and later in the same article it quotes a Wehrmacht officer in Germany as saying, "To me it sounds like awful ingratitude and a mistake. We Germans think now that Mr Churchill is one of the greatest men in the world and if he had been our leader we certainly should not have turned him out after what he has done. It's really most puzzling."

This same edition highlights one of the problems that this might cause. "The new Prime Minister" (Clement Attlee) "will have to take his place without delay at the vital International Conference at Potsdam." This had begun on 17 July between Britain, America and Russia to decide on the details of the occupation of Germany, and as the paper says, "The Conference cannot be expected to remain in recess while Britain chooses a new government." During the earlier stage of this conference Winston Churchill and the new President of America, Harry S Truman, joined together with Chiang Kai-Shek of China to send an ultimatum to Japan for unconditional surrender, which was not heeded at that time.

On 2 August, when the conference finished, the *West Briton* carried the headline, *Historic Meeting. The King's Welcome to President Truman.* "'Welcome to my country Mr President', said His Majesty the King, shaking hands with great cordiality with the President of the USA as Mr Truman stepped on board the British cruiser HMS *Renown*, in Plymouth Sound."

In fact the President had been expected to land in Cornwall, at St Mawgan, on his way back from Potsdam. Arrangements were carefully made here and his plane was tracked across the North Sea, but at the last moment it was diverted to Harrowbeer Aerodrome near Plymouth, no doubt to the disappointment of those in Cornwall. Few knew that President Truman, while at Potsdam had, in great secrecy, ordered the use of the new weapon, the atomic bomb. As he sailed home to the United States on board the cruiser *Augusta*, he heard that it had been dropped on Hiroshima. The date was 6 August 1945.

"A BITTER HAND TO HAND CAMPAIGN"

Victory in Europe had not meant peace for many in the forces. Fighting in Asia had still continued and troops were sent out immediately to reinforce those already there. For many Cornishmen the war was taking them into places they would scarcely have dreamed of. Richard Thomas, the son of a Redruth tin miner, was one of these men and his story can illustrate what happened to many involved in the war in Asia.

After two years of guard and coastal defence duties in England he was sent with his unit, the 2nd Dorset Regiment, out to India in April 1942, sailing in very uncomfortable conditions around the south of Africa. They anchored for a week off Cape Town where they were allowed shore leave. Here he visited, against orders, the home of a black family. He was horrified at the way these people were being treated and was touched to see in their hut a photo of King George VI and to be told, "This is your king, who is also our king."

For many months after their arrival in India they trained, learning about jungle warfare and going on exercises, and then in March 1944, his regiment with the whole of the 2nd Division was sent to north-east India, Assam, close to the border where the Japanese were encamped and trying to cut the rail link between India and China.

They moved through thick jungle, trying to reach Kohima, shooting at anything that moved. "As we were climbing we had to run the gauntlet of sniper fire. I remember running across bodies that had been killed on the way up, my heart pounding." For three weeks they were completely surrounded by Japanese forces, their only supplies being dropped by plane and many of these were picked up by the enemy. "We weren't able to wash or shave for days. We ate iron rations, biscuits and chocolates. It was a bitter hand-to-hand campaign with rifles, Bren guns, grenades and mortars supported by field artillery and later by tanks. But we stopped the Japs coming on into India."

An article in the *West Briton*, written in February 1945 by a military observer, also gives a graphic description of this jungle campaign.

"A single shot rings out - a green-clad figure crumbles and two strong hands grasp him under the arms, hurry him away to the

Victory and Peace 1945

Regimental Aid Post. The little section crouching at the edge of the panjis, those sharp bamboo strips which make a slanting wall of spearheads outside every post in the jungle, continues its vigil. Every man strains his ears to catch the sound of movement; keeps his eyes trained ahead in an effort to detect a sign of the enemy. The only audible sound is the breathing of the man next to him. ...... Ten yards ahead he sees three faces peering above the foliage. A shot rings out. Then a volley from a Bren gun. He drops down just in time. That was three Japs."

Richard Thomas continues. "When we managed to break out our task was to open the road from Kohima to Imphal, 90 miles to the south. They were most demanding days. There were times when we set off in the dark,

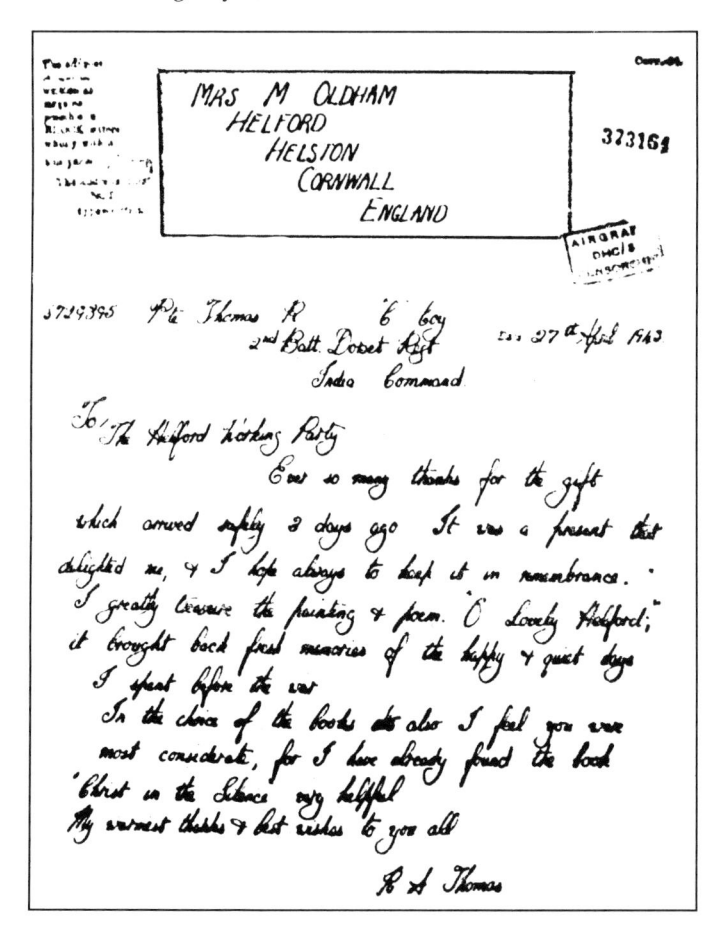

Victory and Peace 1945

with the Japs close by, not knowing what we were going to walk into. If a man stepped on a twig it could immediately alert them and hand grenades would descend on us from all quarters. We got through to Imphal and I can remember even now the tracer bullets bouncing on the roads."

They continued southwards, slowly driving the Japanese forces back through Burma. "I remember crossing a river where we had to cling hold of one another, and then lying up on the other side soaked to the skin, the Japs near by. When we advanced, we reached a village razed to the ground, belongings scattered everywhere. I sat on a heap of rubble in the village feeling desolate." Here in this place so far from home mail reached them, and he received a "Christian Herald", on the front page of which was a text from Isaiah, which cheered him at this time of need. "Though the mountains be removed and the hills be cast into the sea, yet will not my love."

A few days before Victory in Europe was celebrated they at last pushed their way south to Rangoon. Here they were pulled back for a rest to prepare for the next onslaught, the final defeat of Japan. As their plane took off for Calcutta, they were catapulted backwards into the tail. "This old Dakota almost flapped its wings, but we didn't mind because we were going on leave." Within days he was facing death, not because of the enemy, but because of malaria, and while he was slowly recovering, the war was building up to its terrible climax.

Newspapers in Britain had been explaining the developing situation in Asia. On 27 July the *Daily Mail* reported that Allied troops were exploiting the Japanese defeat in Burma and sending out patrols towards the border with Siam (Thailand). Other troops were moving into Northern Malaya, while Japan itself was coming under air attack. Three forces totalling more than 350 Superfortresses dropped 2,200 bombs on chemical and oil targets on the southernmost island. The Allies were closing in, but the Japanese were prepared to fight to the death and this final campaign was expected to be hard and long drawn out with very heavy casualties. It was to bring the war to a quick end that the decision was made to use the first atomic bomb.

The atomic bomb that was dropped on Hiroshima on 6 August killed perhaps 80,000 people on that day alone, and many, many more died from its effects over the next weeks and months. President Truman described it the following day as having "more power than twenty thousand tons of explosives." Experts who studied the photos taken from the air at the time could scarcely believe that the devastation shown was the work of just one bomb.

The *Daily Express* carried the headline: *The Bomb That Has Changed The World*. *This terrific power is packed in a space of little more than golf ball size.*

Victory and Peace 1945

Three days later the *West Briton* had these headlines. *Atomic Bomb. Cornwall and Production of Uranium. Expert's View.* At that stage little was realised by most people of its devastating effects and the paper's article was about the uranium needed for such a bomb. It states, "Whilst no mineral produced in Cornwall was used in making the atomic bomb, the revelation that an essential ingredient is uranium has aroused much interest because Cornwall is the only part of the British Isles where this mineral has been mined in any considerable quantity, though even here it is comparatively rare and has not been produced for years."

The paper also carried another story, that Russia had finally declared war on Japan, "probably the greatest achievement of the Potsdam Conference and the most striking demonstration of the solidarity of the Three Great Powers." But a week later, even after the dropping of the second atomic bomb, this time on Nagasaki on 9 August, the paper has the despairing headline; *The War Goes On. Japan's Surrender Not Yet Made.*

Meanwhile, many people in Cornwall had other and more pleasant things to think about. The Bank Holiday week-end at the beginning of the month had been filled with activity. There were junketings in practically every town and village, from Perranporth Fun Fair to St Columb's Rabbit Show, from Gwennap's first exhibition of cattle and horses to Falmouth's Festival Week, and many, many other events.

Now for the first time for six years families were going away on holiday, although there were still problems. In April the *Daily Mail* had publicised the policy of many hotels refusing accommodation to families with young children because they were "too much trouble." Whether any Cornish hotels followed this line is not reported, but according to the *West Briton* in early August, Cornwall was experiencing a record number of visitors. "Already the local people at the seaside places are marvelling that so many have come so far in search of change and refreshment in spite of the irksome difficulties of travelling, accommodation and food. It is said that one Cornish resident who inserted one small advertisement had over 1000 requests for accommodation."

One such family travelled from their home in Devon by train: mother, father, granny, three young sisters and a cousin, to stay at a guest house in Newquay. Most mornings they would walk through the fields to the cliffs above Lusty Glaze, the air filled with the chirrupping of grasshoppers, then count the steps down to the beach, to paddle, build sand castles, clamber over rocks and play all the usual childish games. But on one day they took a charabanc tour to Bedruthan Steps and it was there that they heard the longed-for news that the war was finally over. Japan had surrendered.

When they returned to their guest house that evening, the tables were bright with colourful paper in wide stripes of red, white and blue,

Victory and Peace 1945

Fancy Dress Parade, Manaccan, VJ Day. *(S. Carter)*

Dancing on the Moor, Falmouth. *(RCPS)*

Victory and Peace 1945

and the rooms were festooned with paper hangings, which on closer examination turned out to be long, twisted strands of Izal toilet rolls. Some people had stock-piled items like this at the outbreak of war, because of the fear of shortages, and now they had been brought out of cupboards and drawers in celebration of the peace.

Once again victory jubilations were the order of the day and similar festivities were re-enacted all over the county just three months after the first rejoicings. Marjory Jones writes: "VE Day was joyful but of course VJ Day, which was celebrated in a similar manner, had that extra abandon. Our war was really over. Broadcasts over the wireless told of the wild scenes in Trafalgar Square and the joy expressed by King George and Queen Elizabeth."

Once again the bunting was flying, the bells pealing, bonfires burning and fireworks exploding, teas were enjoyed in street parties, races run, choirs sang, bands played and the Flora Dance wended its way through streets in St Austell, Lostwithiel, St Columb, St Day, St Dennis, Probus, Newquay, Truro, Helston and in Fowey. Here the day had started with singing in the streets and ended with more singing around a huge bonfire at Squires Field.

Street Party, Berkeley Cottages, Falmouth (RCPS)

Victory and Peace 1945

At Perranporth four huge fires blazed and Chapel Rock was brilliantly lit by incendiaries. Perranwell had a large bonfire on the Green, and a sinister-looking effigy of the Japanese Admiral Togo was paraded around the village in a gaily-decorated handcart, to the accompaniment of motor horns and a megaphone.

In Falmouth events got a little out of hand after people crowded into the streets with bugles, trumpets and bells, because sixteen shop fronts were smashed, flags pulled down and "a tin of spam was thrown through a shop window." At Penzance 3,000 children were entertained with tea, games and sport. At Redruth thousands gathered around the town clock for community singing and at Camborne there was impromptu dancing in the streets.

Celebrations for victory and peace continued over the next few weeks, allowing time to arrange carnivals, street parties and children's games. Thanksgiving parades and services were organised as part of a national savings drive, from a grand parade through the streets of Truro to the quieter open-air service on the beach at the bottom of the steep, narrow streets of Port Isaac.

On 12 September Lord Louis Mountbatten finally received the formal surrender of all the Japanese forces in South-East Asia in the Council Hall of the Municipal Buildings in Singapore. The *Daily Telegraph* correspondent describing the scene, wrote of "an especially precious Union Jack" that was flying over the city. "It was the only one that remained after the British surrender in 1942 and had been hidden in the prisoner-of-war camp at Changi for three-and-a-half years."

A week later the West Briton was reporting news of the first Cornishmen to be freed, who had been in Singapore at that time, and a fortnight later Lt. Hancock, RNVR, of Truro arrived home, one of the first naval POWs to be repatriated. The paper describes him as being remarkably well although he had lost four stone in weight. He told of the time when he was desperately ill with dysentery in the camp hospital, where there was no medicine, and it was one of the medical orderlies, Corporal Tuffery, RAF, of Falmouth, who had helped to save his life by his encouragement and careful nursing.

Stories were beginning to filter through about the horrors of the camps for both civilians and servicemen where, in the hierarchical community of Japan, prisoners were treated badly as others were on the lowest rungs of society. Reports of deaths of Cornishmen in these camps were made in the local paper as Allied forces took over control, and the effects on those who survived could be harrowing and long-lasting.

For most people, exhausted by six years of war, the dropping of the atomic bombs forcing Japan to surrender was welcome. In Truro Cathedral

Victory and Peace 1945

the Assistant Bishop, Dr Holden, said that there were those who saw in the first destructive application of atomic energy to Japan both stern necessity and poetic justice. And he ended his address by saying that properly used "It might well be the greatest of God's material benefits towards them." It was not known then that Japan also had its own atomic bomb programme, although in an early stage.

But not all expressed such views. Even before the end of hostilities, Bishop Hunkin speaking at Gerrans mentioned the appalling forces of atomic energy. He said that it was vital that so terrible a thing must come under responsible control. Frank Pritchard, the Chairman of Cornwall Methodist District, speaking at Newquay asked, "Could we lift up our heads and hearts to God, or must we hang our heads in shame and humble our hearts before the Almighty with a sense of overwhelming guilt?"

Two British men witnessed the dropping of the second atomic bomb from a plane high above the city of Nagasaki, Sir William Penney, the atomic scientist, and an RAF pilot, Group Captain Leonard Cheshire.

10. LEONARD CHESHIRE VC

On 9 August 1945 Leonard Cheshire, one of the most decorated pilots of the RAF, was on a special mission. He was one of two British observers in a huge American Superfortress, who witnessed the dropping of the second atomic bomb on Japan. If this bomb could shorten the war then he was happy that it should be used. It was about 11 o'clock in the morning when the bomb was released and floated down by parachute on to the unsuspecting city of Nagasaki.

Watching it from below was Sidney Lawrence, another British Air Force man. He had been a prisoner of war for nearly three-and-a-half years, working in coal mines and on the roads, expecting to be killed by his guards if the Allies invaded Japan. He saw the falling bomb and then a blinding flash. The earth shook as a wave of suffocating heat, and a tearing blast of wind swept all before it. A mushroom-shaped cloud slowly rose in the air and hung over the city. Then there was utter silence. Shadows of dead people stained the walls of shattered buildings, while many of the living were flayed like butcher's meat. Sidney survived, saved from death by a pile of rubble, and he spent the next numbing hours and days doing what he could to help those who had been his enemies.

The plane Cheshire was in was over thirty miles away when they saw the blinding flash and felt the huge plane rock violently in the blast. A fireball soared into the air, followed by the great mushroom cloud. Cheshire peering through his field glasses, trying to pierce the black smoke, saw the red glow of fires and quickly began to sketch the scene as he perceived it.

This appalling spectacle made a huge impression on him, as with all the American airmen who witnessed it, but unlike some of these men, he continued to believe in the necessity of using this destructive power. In his report he recommended that Britain should stockpile these weapons to keep future peace in the world. However, much of the rest of his life was spent helping people whose lives were shattered. Some of those years were spent in Cornwall.

His war service had been exemplary. He had joined the RAF in 1939, becoming a bomber pilot with various squadrons, being decorated for his successes and rising to the rank of Group Captain, one of the youngest at the time. Later in the war he was posted to the Dam Buster Squadron, training them in high-level bombing to use a new type of penetration

Leonard Cheshire VC

bomb, a tallboy, 12,000 lbs in weight with a reinforced front end. This was so designed that when it was dropped from a height of 20,000 feet it could destroy the massive concrete defences of the German rocket sites. Like the bouncing bombs that this squadron had used earlier, this tallboy was the brainchild of the scientist Barnes Wallis.

While they waited for this bomb to be perfected, the squadron acted as pathfinders for the bombing raids that were now building up prior to the D-Day invasions. The high-level dropping of flares was not very accurate, so Cheshire developed the idea of using a fast, light, manoeuvrable plane that could fly low over the target to drop the guiding flares. The practicability of this strategy had to be proved and after a few successful bombing sorties over sites in France, he suggested an attack on Munich. This city was heavily defended and had not suffered much up until that time, but his tactics, using a Mosquito, proved successful.

With D-Day approaching and the tallboy still not ready, the squadron was deployed in deception, dropping bundles of "window", strips of silver foil, to block German radar and give the impression of an invasion fleet approaching the Calais area. This was to reinforce in German minds the idea that this short route would be the favoured one and not the longer sea crossing to Normandy.

At last by early June, the tallboy bombs were ready for use and Cheshire and his squadron proved their effectiveness by destroying the railway tunnel at Saumur, where several main lines converged. Cheshire in his light Mosquito plane dive-bombed the tunnel, laying his marker flares for the bombers high above, and he witnessed within minutes the collapse of the tunnel and hillside. Important German supply lines to Normandy were now disrupted. E-boat bases in Le Havre and Boulogne suffered next, and then it was the turn of the rocket sites. Huge concrete ramps and bunkers were destroyed but the Germans were already moving back many of the rockets and using deception methods of their own.

After one hundred raids, when statistically he should have been killed four times over, Cheshire was withdrawn from the squadron, and to mark his phenomenal achievements he was awarded a Victoria Cross as well as a third DSO. He then spent two months or so in India, planning bombing attacks on the Burmese jungles, where the retreating Japanese armies were putting up a desperate resistance.

The *West Briton* carried an article which explains the importance of air power here:

"Supplies were brought in mainly by air. Wounded are flown out by Moth planes from strips hacked out of the dense undergrowth by

Leonard Cheshire VC

the auxiliary troops. Casualties have to be carried down sheer precipices to get them to the strips. .....
"The RAF are co-operating nobly. It is hardly credible that among all this mass of evergreen undergrowth they can pick out the right place. Despite it all a Moth has just glided in to take away the first wounded man today. The giant Dakotas are holding off for a few minutes to allow the Hurricane to finish their job and then they too will come in to drop our supplies."

Some time later Cheshire was sent out to the American base in the Pacific on the special mission that climaxed over Nagasaki. This bomber pilot with "a record of outstanding personal achievement," as his citation read, now had to turn his thoughts to the future in a world officially at peace.

The comradeship that the war had created was something that many wanted to try and preserve. Cheshire had a strong feeling for communal help, and for a time wrote articles for the *Sunday Graphic* in which he put forward the idea of co-operation in a community, where the strong would help the weak, the skilled the unskilled, and the rich the poor, until all could cope for themselves. He thought of taking over some of the hundreds of airfields that were now unwanted and use them for settlements. This did not materialise, but it did result in his setting up a home, first in Lincolnshire and then moving to Le Court, in Hampshire. This project soon ran into financial difficulties, but from it grew the first of the Cheshire Homes, where the sick and disabled who had nowhere to go could make a home for themselves.

In May 1947 he was one of the delegates of the United Europe Movement who attended a Congress of Europe at The Hague in the Netherlands. Winston Churchill made a speech on the opening day, calling for Europe to unite "to protect its unique inheritance of freedom". Amongst the politicians, churchmen, writers and other distinguished people who listened to the debates there were some who were concerned over the agnostic and humanist views that were being expressed. Cheshire first publicly showed his ideas on Christian principles in one of these debates, when he criticised humanism just after Joseph Hunkin, the Bishop of Truro, had urged the need to recognise "Christian Humanism". This congress Cheshire regarded as a landmark in his life and he was later accepted into the Roman Catholic Church.

By 1950 Le Court was full and Cheshire, after periods of illness, was advised to take a regular job with a more normal lifestyle. So he joined the Vickers Armstrong organisation to work on a secret project with Barnes Wallis, his wartime acquaintance.

Leonard Cheshire VC

Leonard Cheshire.

Leonard Cheshire VC

This was a revolutionary aeroplane, which was being built and put through a series of trials. These tests were first of all held on an airfield in Bedfordshire, but when the Air Ministry wanted this back, Cheshire was given the job of finding a new test site. The place he chose was Predannack, the isolated wartime airfield on the Lizard Peninsula, where he could enjoy the peace and solitude, but still keep in touch with Le Court, with the use of the two-seater Spitfire, or sometimes a Mosquito, used for testing the range of radio control for the new plane.

Besides doing test flights Cheshire acted as administrator. He had the knack of getting on well with all sorts of people and the organisation ran smoothly under his supervision. "As nice a person as you could hope to find", as one of his colleagues recalls. The airfield was also used by HMS Seahawk, the Royal Naval Air Station at nearby Culdrose, for practising deck landings, but any difficulties here were sorted out by Cheshire who ensured that Wallis' tests did not coincide with Culdrose's use of the airfield.

However he found that there were still people in desperate need of help, and first of all he took into his rented home, near Mullion, an ex-naval frogman who was subject to bad epileptic fits. Later, concerned about the non-appearance of Hilda, who worked in the canteen on the airfield, he went off to look for her home. He found her small, dark hovel, where Hilda was seriously ill with dysentery and her young son in a high fever. He installed them in his rooms on the airfield, and there they stayed for ten days as they recovered.

It horrified him, that at a time when there were so many homeless people, buildings could lie empty, and soon the idea of setting up a second home, this time in Cornwall, began to occupy his thoughts. On the edge of the airfield was a cluster of derelict buildings, now no longer needed by the Air Ministry, and here he planned a new home to be called St Teresa's, after a French nun who had died of tuberculosis (TB) in her early twenties. At first sight the place seemed completely unsuitable. It was filthy with grass growing through the floor, but what made it worse was that there was no drainage, water supply or electricity. But Cheshire was undeterred.

He began to dig drainage trenches himself by hand and a large hole to take the tank he had acquired. The only problem was that when it rained the tank floated as the hole filled with water. Not discouraged by this setback he acquired a larger tank and persuaded a passing excavator from Culdrose to dig the necessary hole, and he then procured a large naval crane to put it in place. Tony Inwards, a colleague of his at Predannack, remembers Barnes Wallis as having a wonderful gift of speech, but Cheshire himself must have been a persuasive talker.

Leonard Cheshire VC

When people knew what he was doing, many came to help him, not only men from the Vickers team but local people as well. Naval men from HMS Seahawk at Culdrose spent some of their leisure time there building a small chapel. Tony Inwards describes Cheshire as having a "frightening conscience", and by this time Cheshire felt that it was wrong of him to be paid for a job which did not require his full attention, and to be spending his time on something different, however worthy, so he resigned from his post with Vickers.

The people of the Lizard adopted St Teresa's and they generously gave help in its early, uncertain days after the new home opened in 1951. One of the first patients, who came from Le Court, died within a few weeks from tuberculosis. He did not want to be buried in the ground, so Cheshire arranged with the Methodist minister at Mullion for a burial at sea. The small cortege negotiated the steep hill down into the fishing cove of Cadgwith. The coffin was placed in a working boat which then chugged slowly away from the beach for the simple, quiet ceremony. This so impressed the boat crew that one was reported as saying, "I'd like to go that way when my time comes."

Some of the residents had mental disabilities and were out of place in a home for the physically disabled. So before long Cheshire had taken over another nearby Nissen hut, converted it, called it Holy Cross and transferred these patients to their new home.

He was constantly on the look for new premises, because he had found a gap that the new National Health system did not fill, the caring for the terminally ill and the disabled with no homes of their own. The ruined medieval church of Ruan Major, hidden behind its shield of trees, caught his eye, with land beside it where a home could be built. This particular idea did not materialise, but a purpose-built Cheshire Home was eventually provided in Cornwall.

The old airfield building used by St Teresa's was unsuitable for the numbers wanting to be admitted and, after a few years, a campaign got under way with the people of Cornwall as a whole adopting the home. With their help, six thousand pounds was raised for a new building overlooking Mount's Bay at Long Rock, close to Marazion, which opened in 1956.

Before all this happened Cheshire had been rushed to hospital at St Michael's in Hayle, where he was diagnosed as having tuberculosis, that all-too prevalent disease of these years, probably caught from one of his TB patients. He went to a sanatorium in Sussex, where it took him over two years to recover, but he had left behind in Cornwall a permanent reminder of his care for others.

11. WILD GOOSE, SWALLOW AND NERVE GAS

During the thanksgiving service for the end of the war in Europe, the Bishop of Truro, Joseph Hunkin, gave thanks for the steadiness and steadfastness of the people "who had rallied to resist the tyrant", and amongst those he listed were the scientists, for their ingenuity. One of the most famous of these was Sir Barnes Wallis, who was in charge of the Research and Development Section of Vickers Armstrong, based at Weybridge in Surrey. He had earlier worked on the design of the R100 airship, and later on the Wellington and Wellesley bombers, but he came to public notice with his invention of the bouncing bomb used in the Dambuster raid of May 1943.

Barnes Wallis had a vision of the future where Britain's position in the world would be maintained by the intelligence, creative originality and the

Barnes Wallis at Predannack (T. Inwards)

Wild Goose, Swallow and Nerve Gas

brilliance of the scientists, who would make goods that were needed and provide "the means of distribution which lie at our doors." He was most interested in achieving long-range, high-speed flight by which Britain could keep contact with the far-flung areas of the world. It was after the war that he began serious trials on a radically new type of aircraft, the Swing Wing Project, the project that Leonard Cheshire became involved with.

The design of this plane, with wings that could move forward for slow landing speed and which would be progressively swept back for higher speeds, eliminated the need for not only the tail plane and elevator but also the ailerons and rudder. This saved about 5% on drag and also saved on the weight of a conventional plane, so that the cargo-carrying capacity of the plane could be increased.

He proved that this could fly by using a model in the wind tunnel at Weybridge, but he needed to demonstrate its manoeuvrability. He had been horrified by the loss of life of air crews following the breaching of the German dams using his unique idea of the bouncing bomb, when fifty three of the one hundred and thirty three men had been killed. He was determined that he would not risk the life of a test pilot, so the trials had to be done by radio control, which made it much more difficult. The early tests were made at Thurleigh Airfield in Bedfordshire in 1949 and early 1950, and it was then that the team moved to Cornwall, following Leonard Cheshire's choice of Predannack Airfield, which was isolated enough to be away from curious eyes.

On this wartime airfield specially-made iron rails were laid, like a railway track without joints, stretching into the distance for half a mile. This carried the launching trolley, on top of which was perched Wild Goose, the model plane with its 25-foot wingspan, named after the Canada Goose which it was thought to resemble. The trolley was propelled along the track at 100 miles per hour or more to launch the plane, which would circle after take off at 80 to 90 miles per hour and fly for five or six minutes, before it landed on the tussocky clumps of heather.

Rockets were used to power both the trolley and the plane, cold motor rockets, which used hydrogen peroxide pumped through silver-plated copper gauze, which then turned into steam with a temperature of 450-500 degrees centigrade. This had to be handled very carefully as it would blow up if in contact with grease or anything organic. The men who fuelled the rockets were dressed from head to foot in protective clothing, the fuel being stored in an isolated hut, which on one memorable occasion the plane managed to crash into on landing. The very first test was carried out late one afternoon, just as the school bus passed by on the Lizard road, and must have caused much excited speculation. This took place in February 1952, but with a model considerably reduced in weight.

Wild Goose, Swallow and Nerve Gas

The first test on the heavier 800-pound model happened two months later. Careful preparations were made, including evacuating nearby people from their homes to dug-outs on the airfield and patrolling the surrounding area. The windy weather was far from ideal, but the plane took off, and guided by the pilot on the ground, turned and completed three-quarters of the circuit at 150 miles per hour, but the landing was misjudged. The plane crashed into a concrete hut and was smashed.

Wild Goose ready for take off at Predannack. (T. Inwards)

Because of accidents like this Wild Goose had to be rebuilt several times, and occasionally there was more than one of these large models available, especially when "top brass" were expected to view the trials.

The team at Predannack was a small one, sixteen Vicker's men supplemented by eight local men, running on a shoestring budget. They were protected from undesirable curiosity by RAF policemen with their Alsatian guard dogs, although security was not usually very tight. The Head of Trials in these early tests was Tony Inwards. He had worked during the war at Weybridge with Vickers Armstrong, on testing the strength of undercarriages of many of the planes used by the RAF, such as the Spitfires and Hurricanes, Beauforts and Blenheims, and then shortly before the war ended he had joined Barnes Wallis in the Research Department. With the end of the war in Europe he worked on the

Wild Goose, Swallow and Nerve Gas

translation of huge amounts of detail acquired from the Germans about their work on rockets. Rocket design was still in its early stages but valuable information was obtained.

Tests like this are always dependent on money, often needing government backing. In 1953 a replacement for the Vickers Valiant bomber was being discussed and Wallis believed that his swing-wing design was better than anything else. His tests led on to the idea of supersonic flight, for which Wild Goose was not suitable. A new model was developed in 1954, called Swallow, with a fuselage redesigned into a delta shape, and from this a piloted model was developed. In 1957 the project finally came to an end as far as Predannack was concerned.

On 1 July 1957, some national newspapers carried a strange story. The headlines in the *News Chronicle* read: *HUSH! One of our aircraft WAS missing.* It then details the story of an "object" from a closely guarded airfield plunging in the sea off the Lizard. It continues, "The scientists wanted it back. Down came the security clamp. First the research men tried to get a boat to sneak out and return at dusk. Then the scientists decided to call out the Lizard lifeboat. All top secret of course. ...... By the time the lifeboat crews reached the lifeboat house the whole village knew that a pilotless plane was in the sea." The lifeboat attempt was then followed by a helicopter search, "But it was the Navy that brought in the secret plane that everyone knew about." However the newspaper report was wrong. Swallow is still lying under the sea off the Cornish coast.

The following year Barnes Wallis and his design team went to the United States to discuss their ideas. The Americans developed the Tornado plane, but having a tail this did not follow Barnes Wallis' design. Perhaps his ideas will yet be developed at some time in the future. Predannack, however, remained in use as an airfield, being taken over officially by RNAS Culdrose in 1959 to practise ADLS, the Assisted Deck Landing Scheme.

Another of the wartime airfields to remain in government hands was Nancekuke, near Portreath, and for a time it came under the control of St Eval as a non-active station. Then in 1950 Nancekuke was transferred to the Ministry of Supply, and soon sinister stories began to circulate. Were skin divers disappearing off the coast of Nancekuke? Why were seals dying in that area? What was the cause of the deformed plants and vegetables that people talked about? Was it sonar signals under the water that caused ear damage to swimmers? Was one of the local men employed there suffering from nerve gas poisoning? What was going on behind that high perimeter fence with its security men and guard dogs?

It is now known that from 1950 to 1978 it was part of the Chemical Research Establishment for research and development connected with

Wild Goose, Swallow and Nerve Gas

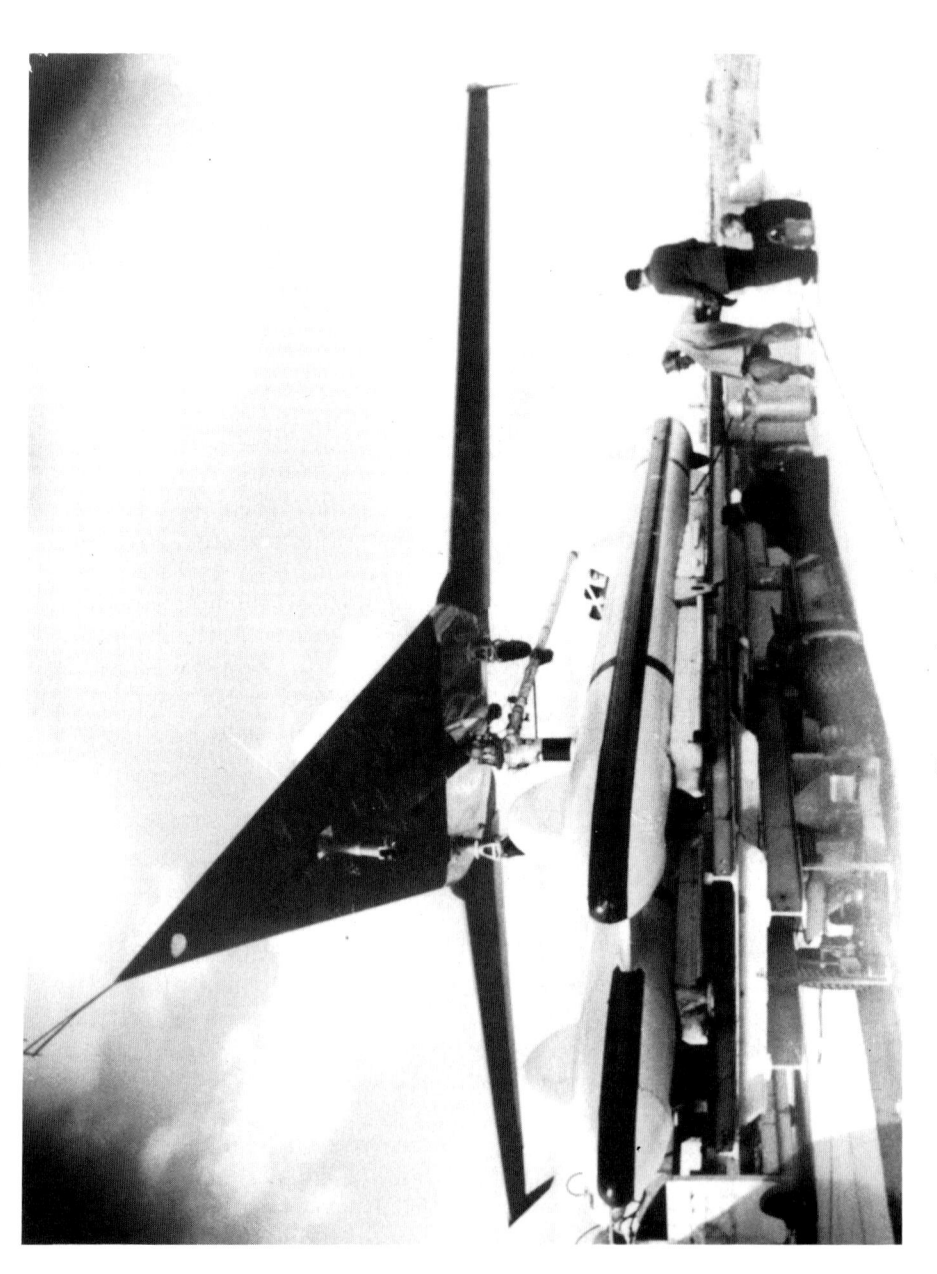

Swallow at Predannack. (T. Small)

Wild Goose, Swallow and Nerve Gas

Porton Down on Salisbury Plain. This in its turn was part of a much wider concern with testing carried out in Canada and Australia and production in America. The violence and destruction of the Second World War had changed the map of Europe, and countries that had once been allies now eyed each other suspiciously in the cold war between the democratic west and communist east. Using chemical weapons could be one way to succeed in any future war.

During the Second World War all the major powers had reserves of chemical weapons to retaliate if they were used by the enemy. Neither side used them. The Normandy campaign or the battle for Berlin might well have led to desperate German attempts to stop the advances by using chemicals, but they did not. Their scientists had produced the first nerve agents, and equipment developed in Germany was brought to Britain after the war, so that tests could be carried out in this country.

Local men were employed on the construction of the buildings at Nancekuke with its administration block, medical block and nerve gas plant containing a bunker with two fifty gallon drums of the lethal chemicals. There was also whispered talk of an undersea pipeline that had cost one million pounds to build.

Here research was done on Charcoal Cloth, Anti-Riot Gas, and the Nerve Gas, Sarin (GB). Some of this work was tried out on people at Porton Down. Ten volunteers a week arrived there during the early 1950s, to be paid one shilling for each test made on them. Since then there have been claims of cancer, sterility and death because of these tests.

None of the work carried out at Nancekuke was openly talked about. Everything was very hush-hush and workers had to sign the Official Secrets Act, so preventing any dangerous leak of information. But many of the local men employed there did not know what they were dealing with. They all carried cards which stated: "In the event of symptoms developing contact the Medical Officer of Health at Nancekuke." These symptoms were "contraction of the pupils and constriction of the chest," and they were given daily blood tests, but not told why.

The symptoms of poisoning by GB are now officially given as starting with a runny nose, then tightness of the chest, dimness of vision and pinpointing of the eye pupils, difficulty in breathing, excessive sweating, vomiting, cramps, twitching and jerking, staggering, confusion, coma and convulsion. Death could then follow. Not a pleasant thought for the workers, if they had known these details.

On 31 March 1958 two local men, who worked there as toxic fitters, were doing maintenance work in a storage cubicle, without any protective clothing or gas masks, which they were told would not be necessary. One of them, Tom Griffiths, noticed a drop of liquid hanging from a pipe and

Wild Goose, Swallow and Nerve Gas

realised there was a leak. They got out quickly, but their eyesight was affected and so was their blood cholinesterase levels. Although they were kept under observation for three weeks they were given no medical treatment.

After this episode, Tom Griffiths suffered from poor memory, variable eyesight, chest pains, and fainting fits, preceded by panic, giddiness and intense heat, and followed by complete exhaustion. It was not until 1969, eleven years after the incident, that the work being carried on at Nancekuke emerged into public knowledge. Compensation of less than £500 was offered Tom, after prolonged negotiations, which was later reduced to £1.75p for loss of vision.

Two years before his accident, in 1956, Britain had officially given up offensive chemical warfare. The Porton Down programme, including the work at Nancekuke, was to be a defensive programme only, concerned with saving lives. But whose lives?

The quiet cliff fields above the sea near Portreath had changed from land worked by a small group of farmers, intent on improving their holdings, to a strategically-important wartime airfield, noisy with fighter planes and bombing, and then to a secret chemical warfare establishment, all within the space of ten years. The war had certainly brought Cornwall into a new age.

12 "NOW WIN THE PEACE"

PROBLEMS OF PEACE

"We have won the German war. Let us now win the peace," said Field Marshal Montgomery on VE Day. He added, "Without doubt, great problems lie ahead. The world will not recover quickly from the upheaval that has taken place. There is much work for each of us."

During the war much of the work, both voluntary and paid, had been done by women, but now, with the men returning, the situation was changing. In March 1945 the *West Briton* expressed what could be regarded as very enlightened views on the position of women. (Although later comments made about the importance of mothers staying at home probably meant that only single women were being considered.) "A world war has once again demonstrated beyond doubt that sex-prejudice is outmoded. ....Experience during the war years has shown that equal rates of pay for women are the best protection for the men's standards. ....As women have been wanted for furthering the war effort so they will be wanted for accomplishing the peace. There is nothing to be gained by denying them the right to use in peace the training they have received in war."

Peace has only begun

Peace has begun—
begun to dismantle
bomb shelters
and road blocks,
mined beaches and wire.
The road signs are back
on the roads of our Island,
the roads that wind safely
to Mother and Dad.
The boys are preparing
for joyous reunions,
for work and careers;
the girls for new homes.

The black years are over,
the grim task is done,
the long war is over,
and peace has begun.
Now on to the future!
New tasks,
new plans,
new problems,
new sowing,
new harvest—
the harvest of peace . . .
For this new beginning,
this mighty New Hope,
this Glorious Opportunity
Let us give thanks.

THANKSGIVING WEEKS

"Now Win the Peace"

Twenty three women had been elected as members of the new parliament, still only a small proportion of the whole, but a record number for all that. The *Daily Mail* stated that it was proud of the talented women journalists it had gathered during the war years and the search was on for new stars. Selected women were being offered free teacher-training under a new emergency scheme, but it was for domestic subjects only with a salary, for those who completed the course successfully, beginning at £270 a year rising in yearly instalment of £12 to £420.

Married women were not encouraged to take up this sort of offer. Work in the home was their future and the *West Briton* highlighted one of their problems: "Wives dreading the return of their husbands after a three to four years' absence." During these war years many women had undertaken work, been given responsibility outside the home, and had become more self-reliant within the home with no man to depend on. They had achieved some measure of independence and confidence which they might be reluctant to lose again.

Many women would have changed and so would their husbands. No wonder there was fear mixed with delight at the thought of their return. For children it could be equally harrowing, having someone who might seem to be a stranger changing the normal routine of the home. Even as early as June 1945 the *West Briton* was commenting that broken homes were among war's greatest casualties. In November 1946 it was reported to the House of Lords that a tidal wave of divorce was sweeping the country, with two-and-a-half times more cases than in 1938, many being couples having had long separations because of the war.

Feeding the family was also a problem for mothers, who had coped with diminishing supplies during the war. But at least the system of rationing and the keeping down of prices was seen to be fair to all whatever class one belonged to. "We did not starve when the country's food stocks were at their lowest and the enemy was sinking our supplies. Rationing saved us." So wrote a member of Helston Women's Institute some years later.

As the war was drawing towards its end the food situation seemed to be slowly improving. In April 1945 the *Daily Mail* carried the story of a record shipment of eggs brought over from Canada which, with four more boats due to arrive, would provide forty distributions of eggs during the year, ten more than in 1944.

The early Cornish potato harvest was also proving to be successful that year with 9,000 acres under production, which according to the *Daily Mail*, would be welcome and "greatly help the anticipated end-of-season shortage." However, potato harvesting was labour intensive and with the

"Now Win the Peace"

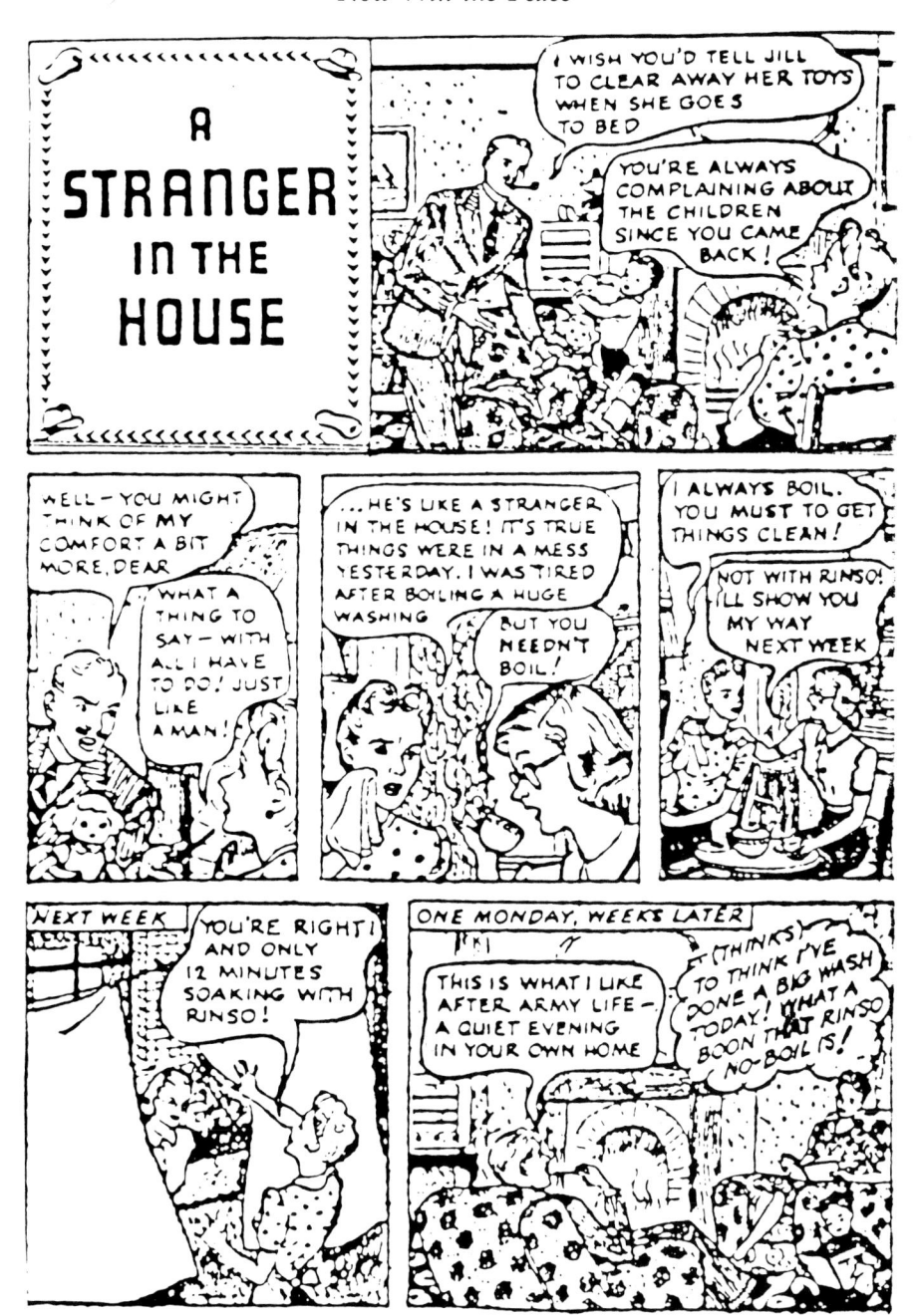

"Now Win the Peace"

men not yet back from the war, and women beginning to leave the Land Army, this could well have proved a problem, as the *West Briton* indicated.

Camps in Cornwall. Volunteer Harvesters Wanted, says a headline on 23 April. The article then goes on to describe five Volunteer Agricultural Camps that were to be set up. The first one to open, on 5 May at Poltair near Penzance, could cater for fifty people a week in a house that was previously a Land Army Hostel, where people were needed for the market gardens. The other four were all to open a month later with potato picking featuring prominently in three of them. Tye Rock Camp at Porthleven could accommodate fifty people a week in a hotel on the sea front, and Rosteague near Portscatho, "with its secret passage - one time smugglers' haunt - running from the house to the sea," could take forty people a week. On a hill overlooking Truro, the now deserted American hutted camp at Polwhele could take sixty people each week, the same number as Hatt Camp at the eastern end of the county, in the fruit growing orchards and fields of the Tamar Valley. Two camps were also to open near Penzance to house schoolchildren to have a working holiday in the country.

By the time the camps had closed for the year in late October or early November the war was over, and after the euphoria of the victory celebrations, people would be hoping for some return to normality in food supplies. However, an article in the women's column of the *West Briton* in early September showed that this was not to be. "A widespread depression is descending on the home front. Women are disappointed at the treatment meted out to them as reward for "services rendered." With their men-folk and daughters on their way home again, the one thing women were looking forward to was more food. Instead we are getting less." Later in the month another article highlights the difficulties for bakers in Falmouth, when cuts in sugar and fat meant that there were constant queues outside shops selling cakes and pastries.

Humour was always one way of combating the problems; the *West Briton* lightened the sombre tone with this joke: *Indignant Customer to Butcher:* "That meat you gave me yesterday wasn't fit for a human to eat. If it hadn't been for my husband's dinner, I'd have brought it back and made you change it."

Rationing was not to end until the early years of the 1950s and in some ways worse was to come before then. Bread rationing began in the summer of 1946 amid newspaper stories of an American bumper wheat harvest, where so much was arriving in Chicago that the grain elevators were choked. However there were areas of Europe worse off than Britain and as President Truman said, "America must continue to share her food during the coming months of hunger abroad."

"Now Win the Peace"

> **BREAD IS LIFE!**
> EVERY GRAIN OF WHEAT COUNTS
>
> **HUNGER FIGHTERS**
>
> YOU CAN—YOU MUST HELP BY THRESHING THE LAST STACKS OF THE 1945 CROP NOW!
>
> **IT'S FOOD FOR OUR PEOPLE**
>
> Help to fill the gap before the next harvest is gathered. All wheat remaining on farms should be threshed at once. If you are in any difficulty get in touch with your Agricultural Executive Committee who will give you every possible help. The country needs your wheat; give it and give it now.
>
> ISSUED BY THE MINISTRY OF AGRICULTURE

The following summer, food rations were cut again because imported foods were heavily restricted because of the dollar shortage. The tinned meat ration was cut to twopence-worth a week, although sweet rations went up from four to five ounces a week and more sugar was being allowed for jam making. In 1949 the sugar ration was cut to eight ounces a week and sweets rationed at four ounces again. But it was difficult for people to accept this situation during peace time, and as Marjory Jones remembers, "Coupons and rationing and above all, shortage of petrol were factors beginning to introduce us to a new Black Market economy."

Fuel of all types was in short supply. In the summer of 1947 the situation became so bad that pleasure motoring was stopped. Domestic coal was sometimes of such poor quality that it was just like dust, not fit for burning. As the *West Briton* said in September 1945: "Another winter is upon us and the prospect is poor - less fuel for heating, less food fuel to keep the cold out, and less wool in which to clothe the shivering body." The Ministry of Fuel was sending out pleas to economise and after the blaze of lights to celebrate peace and victory, darkness set in again, as Truro like many other towns began to restrict the use of street lighting, with most lamps to be extinguished by 11 o'clock at night.

The winter of 1947 might have been exciting for children, with plenty of snow to play with and frozen ponds to slide on, but for their parents the difficulties multiplied. "Snow fall throughout Cornwall during the past week has been the heaviest since the blizzard of 1891," reported the *West Briton* in early February and then, following a short-lived warmer spell, the headline read, "500 Burst Pipes in Truro". A week later there were fears that the gas supplies could run out in the city as the coal supplies were running dangerously low. Some businesses closed early to save fuel and it was to be over a week before the first coal boat arrived.

"Now Win the Peace"

WE KNOW IT'S COLD

BUT don't USE YOUR ELECTRIC FIRE BETWEEN 8 a.m. and 1 p.m.

It's natural to want to turn on the Electric Fire just now — that's what it was made for — to take the edge off the cold snap. Please resist the temptation. Just because it's cold it doesn't mean that the factories don't need the power. The great war effort *must* go on, cold or not. So do a few physical jerks and KEEP THAT FIRE OFF.

Issued in support of the Battle for Fuel, by

CORNWALL ELECTRIC POWER CO.

"Her decks slippery with coal-blackened ice, the 500 ton *Apricity* slipped past the snow-covered fields that slope down to the River Fal and sailed down towards the Channel on Friday's afternoon tide. Behind her at Truro Gas Works men worked among the heaps of coal feeding the furnaces that will give Truro light and heat. Through fog and heavy seas she had ploughed her way from the Humber to the Fal with her high-priority cargo - the first coal to reach Truro since the fuel crisis began."

SPECIAL ANNOUNCEMENT

To assist in lowering the consumption of ELECTRICITY during the remainder of February, the undermentioned Firms will CLOSE at FIVE O'CLOCK each evening, excepting Wednesdays (5.30 p.m.) and early closing day (1 p.m.)

Messrs. N. GILL & SON, Ltd.
Messrs. W. J. ROBERTS & SON.
Messrs. WEBB & Co.
TRURO WEST END DRAPERY STORES, Ltd.

Even in 1951 there were advertisements in the papers for economy in using fuel, with tips to achieve this: *Turn the fire on a bit later, off a bit sooner. Make do with one bar. Turn down the gas. Have small baths. Save hot water. Turn off lights.*

Inflation was another problem to be dealt with. Although government action kept basic food prices down, other necessary goods had risen in price during the six years of war. In 1938 a single bed cost just under £3.10s, (£3.50p) but by 1946 this had risen to £20. Hot water bottles had almost doubled in price, bicycles cost more than double rising from £5 to £12, kettles had trebled in price, vacuum cleaners had risen from £4.10s to £12, while the cost of many clothes had quadrupled. The revolutionary new biro writing pens, advertised to write 200,000 words without refilling, blotting or smudging, went on sale at £2.15s (£2.75p), nearly half an average week's wages.

Disease, want, ignorance, squalor and unemployment were seen as the main evils in the country before the outbreak of war, according to the report to the government by William Beveridge in 1942. This government report quickly became a best-seller, and the recognition of these problems

"Now Win the Peace" did much to raise morale during those difficult years and gave hope for a brighter future once the war was won. War is often a catalyst for changes, accelerating those that have already started and creating an environment for further changes, and this report seemed to show that the necessary reforms would be made.

However, it was the Labour Party's greater willingness to back these plans, enthusiastically supported by many serving soldiers, that won them the election in July 1945. Many men in the forces were fearing peace and the disillusionment of going back to the old way of living. Richard Thomas remembers in Redruth before the war, seeing long lines of men queuing for jobs. As tin mines closed, unemployment had risen and times were very hard. "I can remember my father being given a new pair of boots, which he desperately needed, but he asked me to sell them to get money to buy food."

Biro
MARKS A TURNING POINT IN THE HISTORY OF *Writing*

"BIRO" is unique: it writes with a ball-bearing point—a point that never goes wrong, never floods, bends or splutters—a point that rolls your writing on to the paper with effortless ease. "BIRO" ink dries as you write; you cannot smudge it; you need no blotter.

"BIRO" writes six months or more without refilling—according to the amount you write. To replenish "BIRO" for a similar period of trouble-free service, a refill unit is inserted while you wait.

The demand for "BIRO" has far exceeded production capacity. Consequently you may have to be patient until your turn comes round.

Retail Price 55/- including purchase tax.

"Now Win the Peace"
OPTIMISM FOR THE FUTURE

The war had broken down class barriers to a great extent. Everyone had worked together, coping with difficulties which all had to bear, and it was hoped that this co-operation would continue. On 3 September 1945, exactly six years after the outbreak of war, the *West Briton* carried an article expressing sentiments which explain why some people look back to this time of death and privation with nostalgia. Under the heading, *Community Spirit. No Going Back*, it states; "We don't want to lose the fine spirit of comradeship and friendliness engendered during the blackest years of our existence. What more fitting memorial can we raise to our fellow men who have sacrificed their all, than by keeping alive the comradely spirit of mutual help and understanding?"

There was a spirit of optimism as people were able to enjoy holidays for the first time for many years. The *Daily Mail*, in its unusual eight page edition brought out to publish the election results in July 1945, had an article about the chaos there would be in seaside towns the following summer if something was not done to increase the accommodation available as so many would now want a break. "Families on holiday will have to sleep in converted underground air-raid shelters with blankets issued by the local authority" it warned. It was thought that now there were paid holidays, 26,000,000 people would want to go away from home

Flora Day 1947. Compare this prepared dance with the quickly organised one on VE Day shown on page 110. (S. Carter)

"Now Win the Peace"

compared with 15,000,000 in 1937. To make matters worse, because of the war only 75% of the accommodation used in 1937 would be available.

Going abroad was not envisaged by most people then, so they would have to be catered for in this country. It was suggested that the military camps and American transit camps should be turned into holiday camps with prices of ten or eleven pounds, including fares, for a week's holiday for a family with three children. In due course holiday camps, many purpose-built, became very popular in the post-war years, where everyone joined in together to sample the fun that was laid on for them and where the communal spirit, so noticeable during the war, lived on.

In Cornwall, while some of the camps and war hostels were being used for volunteer farm workers, seaside towns were soon to experience their boom years. The Thomas Cook organisation, well-known in the county before the war, started its package tours again in 1946. It featured ten resorts, seven on the north coast, including Newquay and St Ives, Mullion on the Lizard and Falmouth and Fowey on the south coast The Thomas Cook brochure described Newquay as having abundant facilities and also "mighty promenades in the wild and beautiful headlands framing wide bays fringed with golden sands and washed by the Atlantic rollers." A guide book written after the war states "The town has extended downwards towards the Trenance Valley, and on the other side of the golf links towards Pentire Headland while in a very few years - if indeed such is not already the case - it will be difficult to say where Newquay ends and Porth begins."

However accommodation was not easy in the early post-war years and in some places, such as in the Fowey and Looe areas, there was just not enough for the demand, so that people were recorded as sleeping on guest house floors, in their cars, and even on the seats of buses. One of the reasons for this was that many hotels had been requisitioned for military use. They were gradually made available again, although some needed extensive repairs. The Fowey Hotel had scarcely a pane of glass left intact in the doors after it had been used by the US Navy, but by May 1946 the top floor was ready and soon fully booked. The other reason for accommodation deficiencies was the chronic housing shortage and the problem of obtaining building materials.

The shortage of housing was seen as one of the most crucial problems to be tackled by the authorities. In July 1944 the government revealed its plans to build between three and four million homes in the first decade after the war. These were to have well-equipped kitchens, efficient heating and plumbing and to be built with larger windows and more storage space.

Even as early as August 1943 the *Falmouth Packet* was reporting the approval by the Truro Rural District Council of a post-war housing

"Now Win the Peace"

programme, of 24 more houses for the Mylor/Flushing area, 20 for Feock and 6 for Kea, and in early January 1945, the *West Briton* was emphasising the dire need for housing in the Truro rural area. It was the number of sub-standard houses in Cornwall that created this need rather than the amount of bomb damage. Over half the population of the county had no access to a bath, a third of households had no piped water or exclusive use of a sink. This was much worse than the average for the rest of the country and no wonder American soldiers stationed in Cornwall during 1943/4 had found much of the accommodation "quaint", to put it politely.

Six years after the war, when the new Mayor of Truro, Mr Fred Richards, entered office, he showed that there was still much to do. "I am quite convinced that we shall have to regard housing as priority number one for many years to come." The first post-war houses to be planned in Truro were at Higher Moresk following the Cornish Unit Type design and in 1951 the Mayor was able to report further progress with building under way at Treliske and Malpas.

First of Truro's New Houses

Cornish Unit Type House being built at Higher Moresk, Truro.

Between the two wars houses had often been built strung out in rows, beside the main roads creating ribbon development. Much of the new housing built after the Second World War fostered the idea of community, being built in individual estates or small groups. The *West Briton* frequently reported on progress and discussions on this vital issue

"Now Win the Peace"

and reproduced architects' drawings of their designs and photographs of the finished products.

Even as early as September 1945 St Austell's housing project was "forging ahead", and a month later a photograph appeared of the prefabricated houses on the Thorn Park Estate. Slow but steady progress was reported for the Kerrier area. In Helston an average of thirty-six new houses were built a year both by the local authority and by private enterprise, but in spite of the efforts made there was still a waiting list for accommodation.

Opening of Council Houses at Mawgan-in-Meneage, 1949. (S. Carter)

St Ives boasted the cheapest new houses in the country. The target cost was £900 for a house built as one of a pair, and £850 for those built in a block of four, but in early 1946 a £650 house was proudly on display. So improvements were being made, even if rather slowly.

With the gradual increase in the number of houses came the extension of electricity supplies. A member of Helston WI wrote of how thankful they were to have had electricity during the war. "The drudgery in housework was disappearing and housewives could spare some time each day to help in the war effort." But for many villages and farms these benefits did not come until after the war.

"Now Win the Peace"

One such village was Manaccan, just a few miles away. Walter Eva, the local head of the Auxiliary Forces (the secret army trained in sabotage against a possible German invasion*) lived with his family in a sixteenth century cottage, Woodbine, next to the New Inn. It was lit only by oil lamps and candles. Heat was provided by the open fire in the parlour and the Cornish range, or slab, in the kitchen, which was also used for much of the cooking and for boiling up water. This had to be thoroughly cleaned and black-leaded every week and the brass polished until all was gleaming.

Washday every Monday was a major operation. The "whites" were scrubbed with soap, after soaking overnight, and those still with dirty marks were rubbed on the washboard of corrugated, zinc-plated steel. They were then put to boil in a large, black iron pot, rinsed, "blued", mangled between large rollers worked by a wheel and hung out to dry. This was not the end of the operation as collars and table cloths had to be starched and, if that was not enough, the coloured clothes then had to be dealt with. Dry clothes were then ironed, with either a flat iron heated up on the slab, or a box iron, which was heated by a piece of metal transferred from the slab fire into the box. All the water for this and other household uses, including the outside flush "loo", was pumped by hand from a shallow well outside the cottage.

Five years after the end of the war Manaccan entered the electric age. Poles and transformers with thick wires appeared in the village Bright lights soon shone from windows, electric kettles boiled water, electric irons pressed clothes in next to no time and, luxury of luxuries, electric blankets now began to heat some beds. Electric pumps could now pump pure water from a deep well to the new council houses, the New Inn and Woodbine. Hot water could now pour from bathroom and kitchen taps heated by electricity in the new storage tanks, and indoor toilets were now feasible. This was a revolution in living. New equipment was obviously expensive, with mains radios for example costing £25-£35, so time had to be given to buy the bigger items, but by the mid-fifties the first washing machines began to appear. Monday washday blues started to become a thing of the past. (See Appendix 6.)

Perhaps the greatest worry for many families was the gnawing fear of unemployment. People who remembered the horrors of unemployment and poverty before the war expected a fairer division of the country's wealth after they had fought for victory and peace. In August 1945 the *Daily Express* published the rising numbers of the unemployed, which increased by nearly 23,000 between April and July of that year, but gave the South-West as the area of lowest increase, just twenty-five people.

An article in the *West Briton* in October 1945 discussed the employment prospects in the Penryn and Falmouth area and the need to

"Now Win the Peace"

create some new staple industries or revitalise existing ones. It emphasised the advantages of the enviable geographical position for exporting goods to the western hemisphere by the shortest possible route, and suggested that the docks at Falmouth should develop shipbuilding, which could provide regular employment, to consolidate the repair work already undertaken there.

There was space for new factories and "the adaptable Cornish folk to staff them", but the two big disadvantages in the success of developing new industries were seen to be Cornwall's inferior branch railway systems and the arterial roads "that fail to obviate the congestion of traffic passing through her townships."

The article ends: "the past few years proved we were neither bankrupt of ingenuity nor ability to achieve the almost impossible in the prosecution of a successful war. Cannot the same skill and drive be directed to the exploitation of industry?"

The Camborne/Redruth area seemed once again to be about to suffer from high unemployment. In October 1945 East Pool tin mine, which had once employed 350-400 men, closed leaving South Crofty as the only mine working in that immediate area. But over a year later the *West Briton* was able to headline: *A Good Year. Unemployment Negligible in Camborne/Redruth.* It reported that there were probably fewer people registering for work, i.e. unemployed, than at any time during the previous thirty years.

There were two reasons for this. One was the engineering works in the area: Holman Bros, Camborne and Climax Rock Drill Engineering Company, the Carn Brea Company and Messrs Bartle also of Carn Brea. The second reason was the greater mobility of the work force as road traffic built up again after the war, because the article highlights the lengthy journeys undertaken by many men to get to work.

Some of these probably found work in the expanding china clay industry around St Austell. As early as October 1945 the demand for china clay was outstripping their output because of labour shortages. Under the management of Sir John Keay, this industry widened its products to produce, for example, materials for pre-fabricated housing. The *West Briton* had a photograph, in February 1946, of a specimen China Clay Sand "Unit" house, which was an all-Cornish response to the shortage of both houses and the materials for building new ones.

At Helston, the development of the new Royal Naval Air Station at Culdrose brought development to the town, both in the form of houses and roads and in the need for service trades. So the employment opportunities, not only here but also in other parts of the county, were quite bright, although still not as favourable as for the country as a whole. In the later

"Now Win the Peace"

1950s, according to statistics by the Helston WI, the average percentage of unemployed people in Cornwall was about 3-4%, compared with 1-2% in Great Britain as a whole.

Besides the prospects of a job and better housing there were other dramatic changes taking place. The one aspect of the Beveridge Report which was not very controversial and was put into motion before the war ended, was the change in education. By the Butler Education Act of 1944, the school leaving age was raised to fifteen, made official in 1947, and all children were to have the opportunity of a secondary education. This was to be either at the existing grammar schools or in the new county secondary and technical schools and no fees were to be payable at any of them.

Village schools began to lose their older pupils, who now needed to be bussed into the nearest town, where schools were being moved into bigger premises or later housed in completely new buildings. At Helston, for example, apart from a private school and the Grammar School, there had been two schools that had catered for children from five years old to fourteen, the Council School and the Church of England School. From 1946 the Council School ceased to exist, but its buildings were used for the new County Secondary Modern School, for those children who did not go to the Grammar School at the age of eleven. The buildings of the Church of England School, which had been divided into two departments, now became the Infants School, for five to seven year-olds in the old boys' department, and the old girls' and infants' department now became the new voluntary Primary School for seven-to eleven-year-olds.

The West Briton's headlines in October 1945 pick out the main aspects of these changes. *A Huge Bill. Seven Million Pounds for Education. Cornwall Education Development Plan.* It then ends with perhaps the most important change; *Equal Opportunities For All.*

The other huge change that was to help break down class barriers and treat people more equally was the introduction of the National Health Service. The Liberal Government had laid limited foundations for this in the early years of the century, but by this new scheme, which came into force in 1948, all medical, dental and optical treatment was to be made available for everyone, to be paid for by taxation. Within twelve months 95% of the population had joined the scheme.

Before this time many people had put off visiting their doctor because of the payment involved. Doctors fixed their own charges and patients had to buy everything they needed. It was possible to contribute to a Nursing Association; at Helston this cost five shillings a year in 1939, which seems negligible today, but when the average wage was about £2 5s, it was a considerable amount for people to budget for and many paid in weekly instalments. For this, general cases involving the District Nurse were free,

"Now Win the Peace"

Manaccan Elementary School, 1949; still an all-age school. (S. Carter)

"Now Win the Peace"

but for a confinement a charge of £1 6s was made. If a subscriber had not paid his or her full 5s then a charge of 2s a visit was made, with £2 payable for a confinement.

A Helston WI report made in 1959, just over ten years after the new National Health Scheme began, states "There is no doubt that the health of the people of Helston is well cared for, especially since the new Act, and the only thing which causes inconvenience and sometimes discomfort is the distance a patient or mother-to-be must travel for examination at a hospital."

Early in 1946 Aneurin Bevan, the Health Minister, spoke of improvements in illness and death rates in the country, but that tuberculosis was one of the main problem areas along with venereal disease. The Helston WI report also highlights measles, but tuberculosis was shown as the worst infectious disease. Three people died from the lung disease in Helston in 1949, giving a death rate slightly higher than the national average. St Just-in-Penwith had the highest rate in Cornwall per head of population, with Penryn coming second, according to a report early in 1951. This was seen as a result of the war, with 40% of the cases in Penryn being infected by evacuees and forty-seven of the cases being contracted while on active service.

Dairy cattle could carry the germs and pass them on through the milk, so regular testing of cattle for the disease began. Milk that was clear of the disease was sold separately as TT (tuberculin tested) milk and cattle markets, like Helston, had special buildings to keep TT cattle segregated from the others.

When Marjory Jones finished her nursing training at the Royal Infirmary in Truro at the end of the war she went to the Isle of Wight to nurse patients with chest conditions, especially tuberculosis. She was warned by a senior nurse before she left Truro, "The sadness of it. And you love them so. They're practically all young and beautiful and there is nothing to do except to cry with them." She found this true and many of her patients were ill because of the deprivations of war. The women patients on arrival were in a far more advanced stage of the disease because of their stoicism, caring for their families until they were forced to give in and go for treatment.

The only treatment then was plenty of fresh air, rest, and months of convalescence, with gradually more exercise being taken, which was why hospitals that specialised in this illness, like Tehidy near Camborne, were situated in the country where the air was pure. (Tehidy Hospital had opened as a war memorial in 1919 for tuberculosis sufferers.)

However one good effect of the war was to speed up some areas of medical research. Marjory witnessed the first use of streptomycin on a

"Now Win the Peace"

young girl suffering from a fatal form of meningitis caused by the tubercle. This new antibiotic had not been through its proving period, but the little girl was given daily doses for many weeks and finally recovered. In due course this became an accepted treatment for tuberculosis.

With the coming of the National Health Service, more preventative measures became widespread. From 1949 Helston records show an increasing number of children were being immunised against diphtheria and later whooping cough and poliomyelitis, so that many childhood killer diseases were being almost eliminated.

The other new "miracle" cure that was developed during the war was penicillin. This had no effect on tuberculosis but had amazing curative properties on many other infections. Cornwall played its part in this, because of special seaweed, gonothyraea, which could be collected from the rocks when the tide was very low. From this agar-agar could be extracted and used in the culture of penicillin. Before the war these supplies for research had come from Japan, so during the war Cornish beaches were able to provide a vital ingredient. In February 1945 the *West Briton* reported that twenty-one tons had been collected in Cornwall the previous summer. Supplies of the drug were limited and the demand was great, as shown by the court martial of an American army doctor in Paris two months later, charged with selling it on the Black Market for £20 a tube.

Marjory Jones again witnessed the power of this new medicine before she left Truro. A nursing friend of hers became dangerously ill with osteomyelitis which developed into general septicaemia. She was in agonising pain and death seemed near. But someone in authority contacted Oxford, where the tests on the new drug were being carried out, and supplies were sent to Truro. Her friend responded to the treatment and recovered.

However, this drug was still only in the experimental stage. Corporal Roy Skinner of Helford was wounded soon after D-Day and was given this "wonder" drug. He was soon being flown back to a hospital in Britain direct from the beach-head, not because of the wound but because of his violent reaction to the medication. But for many people penicillin proved to be a life-saver.

Marjory remembers the respect with which it was treated in hospitals, when at last it became more generally available. She was a theatre sister then and very strict procedures were followed. Even if she was in bed she would be called to collect it from the refrigerator and then carefully check the dose with the nurse on duty.

So by 1951, six years after the end of war and halfway through the century, it really did seem to many people that those ills of society, disease, want, ignorance, squalor and unemployment were, if not eliminated

"Now Win the Peace"

completely, well on the way to this goal. In spite of shortages and rationing, fighting against communist forces in Korea and the lurking fear of atomic destruction, people could feel some optimism for the future, so that an extravaganza, the Festival of Britain, suited the mood of the moment.

POSTSCRIPT - THE FESTIVAL OF BRITAIN

"The First Outstanding Operatic Event of the Festival of Britain". This was the advertisement in the *West Briton* in January 1951 to publicise the first amateur performance in the country of the musical "Bless the Bride" that had been entrancing London audiences with its melodies and romance. Truro was entering into the spirit of this year, the halfway point of the twentieth century, the year when the government sponsored the brilliant extravaganza of entertainment and light on the South Bank in London. "The people giving themselves a pat on the back," as Herbert Morrison, the Home Secretary, explained.

> The First Outstanding Amateur Operatic Event of the
> ## FESTIVAL OF BRITAIN YEAR
> at the
> ## REGENT THEATRE, TRURO
> WEEK COMMENCING 5th FEBRUARY.
> The Truro Operatic and Dramatic Society will have the honour to present
> **THE AMATEUR PREMIER FOR GREAT BRITAIN**
> of the Highly-popular Musical Show
> ## "BLESS THE BRIDE"
> (by arrangement with Samuel French Ltd).
> Book and Lyrics by A P Herbert   Music by Vivian Ellis.
> Each Evening at 7.15 p m   Matinees Wednesday and Saturday at 2.30 p m
> Prices of Admission ---7/6. Numbered and Reserved; 5/-, Reserved; 3/6 (obtainable on day of performances only) No 3/6 available Friday and Saturday nights
> Booking at the Regent Theatre only commences Jan. 22nd, 10.0 to 12.30, and 2.30 to 4 p m. daily. (Patrons, Jan. 18th to 20th).   No telephone bookings.
> Vice-presidents and Patrons may obtain vouchers entitling them to priority bookings of numbered and reserved seats for this production from the Honorary Business Manager, E. J. JOLLIEF, 6, Pydar-street, or Members of the Society NOW !
> COME EARLY IN THE WEEK AND AVOID DISAPPOINTMENT.

Exactly a hundred years earlier, in 1851, London had hosted the Great Exhibition, made memorable by the glittering creation of the Crystal Palace celebrating the industrial and colonial pre-eminence of Great Britain. Now,

Postscript - The Festival of Britain

after two horrifying world wars, Britain's industries were struggling and her colonies were mostly independent, but the people needed to be able to forget their troubles and the austerities, still too much in evidence, and not only enjoy themselves but also look forward to a brighter future.

The bomb-destroyed south bank of the Thames was transformed into an exhibition site, brilliant at night with the floodlit Dome of Discovery, and the elongated Skylon seemingly floating in the air. Just as the Cornish steam packet and stage coach services had offered reduced fares in 1851 for the Great Exhibition, so in 1951 the long-distance coaches, Royal Blue, were offering a special night service from Cornwall to London to see this brilliant sight. The centrepiece of the exhibition was the Royal Festival Hall, designed and built for the occasion, and the only building to remain after the festival closed in September.

Representatives from Cornwall were invited to the opening in early May, when the Mayor of Truro, Mr Fred Richards, with six others from the Duchy attended the impressive service of dedication in St Paul's Cathedral. This was followed by the official opening by King George VI and they were later entertained in the Mansion House by the Lord Mayor of London.

Although the South Bank of London was the main focus for this festival, which included a funfair at Battersea, all areas were encouraged to "do their bit" to make this year a special one. Truro opened the festival a few days earlier than the capital, with its own parade and inaugural service in the cathedral, and the Mayor linked the festival to his attempts to provide specially built homes for the aged.. Falmouth promised to "make the town as beautiful as possible with flowers during the summer months." Penzance celebrated with a performance of Haydn's *Creation* by the Choral Society, made special by the well-known soloists who joined them, including Owen Brannigan and William Herbert.

More prosaically Helston Borough Council suggested a new entrance to Porthleven beach, as part of their festival plan, and Helston Town's own celebrations had an extra edge as it was seven hundred and fifty years earlier that their town charter had been first granted.

St Ives Society of Artists held a Festival competition, where "a colourful painting of Nancledra" gained the first prize. But earlier the town had the chance to see the statue that dominated the platform of the Dome of Discovery in London. This huge sculpture, Contrapuntal Forms, was carved by Barbara Hepworth in her studio in the town.

The Festival ship, *Campania*, toured the coast during the summer, calling at Plymouth in early July. Parties of schoolchildren descended on the town for the occasion, but for one twelve-year-old at least, the day was made most memorable, not by the exhibitions on board, but by the train journey there and the exciting boat trip round the harbour gazing up at the

Postscript - The Festival of Britain

impressive hulls of naval vessels as spray showered over the excited children.

What would the next fifty years of the twentieth century be like? A week after the opening of the Festival, the first hydrogen bomb was tested successfully by the Americans on a Pacific island, far more powerful than the atomic bombs that had destroyed Hiroshima and Nagasaki. United Nations armies were already fighting against communist forces in Korea, so the fear of a third world war with the use of "the bomb" was palpable during this time. Space exploration had not yet begun, but the *West Briton* carried an article in January 1951 stating that there was already a waiting list for the first passenger-carrying rockets to Mars. Scientific advances were escalating rapidly in an exciting way, or was it frightening? Would those ills of society, disease, want, ignorance, squalor and unemployment be finally defeated? Only time would tell.

FESTIVAL SHIP 'CAMPANIA'

Aboard the 16,000 ton Festival Ship 'Campania', converted aircraft carrier on loan from the Admiralty, the biggest floating show ever produced is visiting Plymouth. It tells the same story as London's great South Bank Exhibition -- the contribution to civilisation of the Land and the People of Britain — but in its own exciting way. Among the thrilling new displays are a radar installation showing a moving picture of the port itself; models of an Underground railway junction and London Airport as it will be when completed; a jet engine and a seaside pub; several full-size boats and working models of busy shipping ports. This is Plymouth's great Festival show — the one you mustn't miss!

seaborne exhibition visits PLYMOUTH

WEST WHARF • MILLBAY DOCKS

JULY 5—14

ADMISSION 2/-

CHILDREN 5-15 (not admitted unless accompanied by an adult) 1/-

APPENDIX

Since the publication of *Operation Cornwall 1940-1944* last year, more details have come to light, and some of this information is included below.

1. The Tragedy of the *Lancastria*.

In June 1940 British troops were evacuated not only from the beaches of Dunkirk, but later in the month after the fall of France, many more were also evacuated from the areas around Cherbourg and St Nazaire. This was also the time when hundreds of civilians poured on to any boat they could find to escape the advancing German army. Many of these people found refuge in Falmouth, including some of the servicemen who survived the destruction of the *Lancastria*. Although people in Falmouth knew that a ship had been attacked, the details were not generally known. The following is part of a letter we have received from Mr A G Benson of Shepherds Bush, London.

The Lancastria was not torpedoed on the way home from France, but was bombed and sank at anchor off St Nazaire during the late afternoon of 17 June. I can confirm that as I was one of the survivors. There were some five to seven thousand personnel drowned, with about one thousand to twelve hundred survivors. The official figures were never known as nobody was sure how many boarded the ship in the first place. Mr Churchill had the news of the disaster suppressed at the time, and it was the survivors who first made it public during July. I was among the survivors who were taken to Plymouth, where we landed on 18 June at night.

2. Special Construction

The Company of Harbour and General was appointed to prepare beaches for the embarkation of vehicles and troops for D-Day. The name given to this contract, whose purpose at the time was top secret, was Special Construction, a suitably vague name. Mr E Russell had the overall responsibility for building these hards at the eleven chosen sites from Brixham westwards. There were four in the Falmouth area: at Grove Place in Falmouth, Turnaware and Tolverne on the River Fal and Polgwidden Beach at Trebah on the Helford. He writes:

Appendix

The contract required the preparation of the beaches down to the lowest spring tides to enable tanks and military vehicles to run across the beaches, and the construction of three or four dolphins out into the water to enable tank landing ships (LSTs) to tie up to them whilst the tanks, vehicles and troops could embark from the prepared beaches.

The short time available for the contract necessitated planning its execution in great detail. The pile driving equipment had to be specially designed to meet the particular requirements at each site. The ship repairing yards at Falmouth, Fowey and Devonport played an important role here and were particularly helpful in completing this essential equipment urgently.

The main material requirements were the long timber piles, and the country had to be scoured to find the number of piles of adequate length. Licences were necessary to obtain cement, fuel and other such items in short supply.

The preparing of the beaches and the laying of the concrete blocks were very much dependent on the state of the tides. These were studied in great detail on a daily basis and the work planned accordingly, including varying the hours of work to lay blocks at very low tides. On two occasions bulldozers were trapped on a rising tide and had to be rescued.

The pile driving for the dolphins called for skill and experience in positioning the piles accurately during the varying weather and tide conditions, particularly at Trebah where heavy seas were frequently encountered.

At Trebah two ladies lived in the house and were in the habit of taking an early morning bathe from the cove every day. They were naturally distressed when they were informed of the work to be carried out at their beach, but they arranged to continue for some weeks until this eventually became impossible.

3. American Forces and D-Day

F Company of the American 175th Infantry Regiment (29th Division), was based for the last months leading up to D-Day at Porthleven. The Commanding Officer, Captain Robert Miller, with his command group and two platoons, lived at Pendarves House. The third platoon was billeted at the Tye Rock Hotel, Porthleven. (See Page 138.) The men spent the time in training, including rifle practice, road marches and amphibious exercises, and took part in Operation Duck* aboard LST 372, landing at Slapton Sands on 2 January 1944.

On 17 May 1944, they moved to the marshalling area to prepare for Operation Overlord. Their "sausage" (long, narrow camp beside the main road) was on the Falmouth-Helston Road between Trewennack and Rame Cross. Here the officers were given a complete picture of the whole operation, with details of the number of boats, the units involved and the air cover to be provided. Rubber relief maps and aerial photos were used to familiarise them with the terrain. The officers then fully briefed the men

Appendix

in their units. On 1 June most of the regiment loaded on to the LSTs, with F Company embarking on LST 28, which was under the command of Commander Bryan Quirk.

At the time of the fortieth anniversary of D-Day, Captain Miller wrote to Commander Quirk, and extracts from this letter are given below.

On the Near Shore, at Falmouth, England, in early June 1944, you embarked 659 troops for Operation Overlord. It was to be the supreme effort of the Western Allies to invade German-held Europe.

The troop units aboard were an Assault Company and a Support Company of the 29th Infantry Division, sixteen detachments from various other units, the 67th Evacuation Hospital, and a section of the 320th AA Balloon Battalion (complete with cable-towed balloon), plus all the combat vehicles and equipment of the various units.

The troops were bound for the Far Shore and D-Day 6th June in Normandy. The mission of LST 28 and her crew was to land us on Dog Red One Beach near Vierville-sur-Mer, and my mission was to get ashore, blast through the beach defenses and fight our way to the 2nd Battalion assembly area at Gruchy village. ...... My people were armed to the teeth with a large assortment of murderous weapons and demolition explosives, and we made use of them as we went about our professional work.

You billeted and fed our people in constricted and most difficult circumstances, but it was the kindness and concern of you and the crew which we have never forgotten. Your people went all out to help us, for which I offer my most sincere thanks. ....

Thanks to you and your people, I landed five officers and 206 men on Omaha beach. Two of my lieutenants were killed and two wounded; 33 men were killed, 134 wounded and 11 missing in the Normandy Campaign. Only 28 exhausted survivors reached our final objective, the ruined town of St Lo. And, after Villebaudon, they too became casualties. .... I was the last commissioned officer left when my luck ran out. I spent two years in eleven different hospitals; France, England and Stateside. ...... So, after forty years, as D-Day 6 June 1944 anniversary approaches, I think of Bryan Quirk and the people of LST 28. We Infantrymen grow old now, but we do not forget our naval comrades.

One of the casualties was Staff Sergeant Sherwood Hallman, who had been in Porthleven. He was wounded three days after D-Day, but was able to return to his unit. During the assault on Brest he won America's highest honour, the Medal of Honour, but was killed the following day.

Top Sergeant Harvey Folks of B Company, who had been based at the Godolphin Hotel, Marazion, was luckier. He had married a local girl, Mary Martin, only a few days earlier in All Saints Church, had then

Appendix

embarked with the 175th rear echelon at Southampton on 5 June and survived the campaign. He and his wife celebrated their Golden Wedding on 27th May 1994.

4. The Return of the *Mutin*

The *Mutin*, which had left the Helford River in the autumn of 1942 (Chapter 2) for undercover work in the Mediterranean, returned two years later. Tom Long, one of the crew, recalls: "From Gibraltar we did well until we ran into the Daddy of all storms off Cabo de Sao Vincente. Reefing right down we just had to sit and ride it out on a home-made sea anchor. I had great faith in the sea-going qualities of *Mutin*. My dear friend Pierre (Guillett),* once told me that it had been designed on the shape of a seagull." As the storm eased to a heavy swell they crossed the Bay of Biscay with little sight of stars or sun to help in navigation.

The sailor at the wheel, Bill Turner, recalls: "It was pitch dark. The Skipper said we would see in two hours time two red lights ahead, and that would be Falmouth. And they appeared, dead on time. We were met by the Boom Ship with the question, 'Where have you come from?' When we said 'Italy', they rolled about laughing. If they had known what a wonderful ship *Mutin* was they would not have been so amused." They dropped anchor there for the night and then the following morning they moved off to the Helford River. *Mutin* was home again.

Some time later they sailed her back to France. Bill Turner takes up the story. "We had to wait our turn at the Caen Canal. Going up the canal was quite a sight, going through Pegasus Bridge, by the land that was first liberated by the Airborne Troops. At Caen we were met by the French people who were taking her over. They were so pleased with the condition of the ship."

Today *Mutin* is used for training, and she is the oldest of the ships to sail under the flag of the French Navy.

5. The Secret Army

The story of these local units, raised to act as saboteurs on the German forces if they had invaded the country, has been told in *Operation Cornwall 1940-1944*. They were disbanded in the autumn of 1944 and in the *West Briton* in January 1945, a photo appeared of Captain Abbiss, who had organised a unit on the Roseland Peninsula, and in the last months had taken responsibility for all the Cornish units. The caption below the photo reads: *Capt. H W Abbiss, DCM, MM, of Truro, who has been awarded the MBE (Military Division) for meritorious service in connection with a specialised branch of Home Defence.* Even then no hint was given as to the real nature of his work. Secrecy was still important.

Appendix

6. The Lavatory before the Flush

Memories of "Woodbine", Manaccan before the post-war improvements. This account by the Rev. Nigel Eva arrived too late to include in Chapter 12, but it explains why many of the Americans based in Cornwall found the living conditions "quaint."

Today we take the flush toilet in the house totally for granted. At any time of day or night it is there, available within seconds, reasonably warm, with its own light. The contents are washed away beyond our care. But within living memory many homes had no drains or piped water.

We had a reasonably substantial stone-built shed, discreetly at the far end of the garden. It was fitted with a wooden bench against the wall, of two heights - to suit children and adults - with holes to match. The products simply dropped on to the ground some two feet below. Eventually the build-up had to be cleared out with a long-handled Cornish shovel, the householder simply shovelling out the accumulation through a space at the back, and then burying it in a shallow trench in the garden. The fertility of the garden was thus increased generation by generation.

It served its purpose well enough when it was daylight and fine weather. But it was decidedly not all right if it was pouring with rain, and you had to make a thirty-yard dash to the far end of the garden. Worse still at night, if you did not have a torch, and had to find your way by feel to the dark entrance, find the candle, and light it with the (probably damp) matches.

And worse still again, if a storm was blowing off the Atlantic, roaring remorselessly through the tall elm trees, guttering the candle and making the shadows dance menacingly in the far corners, and even blowing the candle out altogether.

Small wonder that as children we were reluctant to venture out there at night. Mercifully there was, of course, the alternative provision - the chamber pot, one under each bed.

What finally ended the reign of the earth closet was my grandmother. She lived in Helston, where she had a modern water and toilet system (and bright, bright, gas light). She refused to come to stay until something was done. So in another slightly nearer shed, my father provided the modern wonder of the age: a chemical Elsan lavatory.

BIBLIOGRAPHY

Air Ministry Publication 3368 1963 HMSO
(Anon.) 1994 *A Brief History of RAF Portreath* Bridge Publishers
Birkin D. *The L'Aber Wrac'h Saga*
Branfield J. 1972 *Nancekuke* Gollancz
Derrien J-F. *Gendarme et Résistant*
Boyle A. 1955 *No Passing Glory* Collins
Dumais L. 1974 *The Man Who Went Back* Future Publications
Braddon R. 1975 *Cheshire VC* White Lion Edition
Freeman R. 1994 *A Wren's-Eye View of Wartime Dartmouth*
                          Dartmouth History Research Group
Graves C. *The Thin Red Lines* Standard Art Book Co.
Hart C.S. 1990 *Cornish Oasis* The Lizard Press
Hughen R. 1993 *Par les Nuits les Plus Longues* Coop Breizh
Hartcup G. 1970 *The Challenge of War* David & Charles
Hume S. 1946 *Operation "Marie Louise"* Blackwoods Magazine No. 1567
Jane's 1988-9 *NBC Protection Equipment*
Landry E. 1978 *Memories of Nancekuke* Landry and Branfield
Eds. Mattingly & Palmer 1991 *From Pilgrimage to Package Tour*
McCormick & Perry *Images of War* Orion Books
Ed. Mercer D. 1988 *Chronicle of the 20th Century* J.L. Int. Public
Nissen J. 1987 *Winning the Radar War* Robert Hale
Packer J.E. *The Spies at Wireless Point* Porthcurno Paper No. 16
Ed. Payton P. 1993 *Cornwall Since the War* Instit. of Cornish Studies
Pickles H. 1994 *Untold Stories of Small Boats at War*
Remy *Mémoires d'un Agent Secret de la France Libre*
Putley E.H. 1985 *The History of the RSE* The Institute of Physics
Richards & Reynolds 1994 *Fowey At War*
Sigmund E. 1980 *Race Against the Dying* Pluto Press
Spath F. 1977 *How the Cheshire Homes Started* L. Cheshire Foundation
Sweetman J. 1982 *Operation Chastise* Jane's
Vyvyan C. 1952 *The Old Place* Peter Dalwood
Walford E. 1989 *War Over the West* Amigo Books
Wood D. 1976 *Attack Warning Red* Macdonald and Jane's

INDEX

Illustrations in italics

Airfields 87-103, *88*, *91*, *94* See also PORTREATH, PREDANNACK, ST EVAL, ST MAWGAN, ST MERRYN.
Air raids 10, 12, 14, 21, 22, 39, 50, 54, 62, 67, 73, 78, 80, 84, 88, 90, 107, 116, 123, 129, 156
Atom Bomb 78, 114, 116-7, 121-2
Auxiliary Units 146, 159

Belgium (Belgian) 20, 107
Beveridge Report 140, 148
Bodmin 60, 80, 97, 109
Brittany 23, 25, 27, 31, 36, 39-40, 43-5, 50, 54, 95, *42*, *46*
    Brest 42, 45, 80, 88, 90, 96, 97, 158
    Concarneau 31
    L'Aber Wrac'h 43, *42*
    Landeda 40, 46, 48, *47*, *48*
    Landernau 40
    Lannilis 40, *42*, *46*
    Lorient 29, 32, 95
    Plouguerneau 40
    Pont Aven 27, 33
    St Nazaire 31, 39, 52, 97, 156

Cable & Wireless See PORTHCURNO.
Cadgwith 127
Callington 80
Camborne 82, 102, 120, 147, 150
Cheshire, Leonard 121, 122-7, 129, *125*
Coads Green 82
Constantine Bay 55
Coverack 67, 70, 75, 81, 92, 95
Culdrose 103, 126-7, 131, 147

Dam Busters 122, 128-9
Dartmouth 29, 31, 35, 39, 52, 54
Davidstow 87
Devoran 112

Dry Tree 66-7, 80
Dutch 103, 124

Eisenhower, Dwight 14, 77, 99
Employment 22, 52, 140-1, 146-7, 151, 155
Exeter 84

Falmouth 10, 12-6, 20-1, 23, 25, 31, 35, 39, 41-4, 47, 50, 52, 56, 88, 92, 107, 112-3, 117, 120, 138, 143, 146-7, 154, 159, *118, 119*
Fal River 10, 12-4, 16-7, 58, 104, 140, 156, *9, 11*
Farming 136, 138, 143
Feock 104, 112, 144
Ferry Boat Inn 18-26, 50, *19-21, 26*   See also HELFORD.
Fowey 50, 119, 143, 157
France 10, 17, 20, 29, 31, 35-6, 39, 52, 60, 66-7, 84, 86-7, 99, 106, 123, 156, 158-9.   See also BRITTANY.
   Bruneval 31, 72
   Caen 159
   Cherbourg 20, 40, 156
   Normandy 10, 16-7, 78, 84, 86, 99, 104, 106, 123, 133, 158
   Omaha Beach 10, 16, 104, 158, *15*
   Paris 10, 39-40, 45, 62, 75, 106, 151
   St Lo 158

Glendurgan 18
Goonhilly 66-7, 70, 78
Grampound 108
Gwennap 117

Hayle 127
Health 127, 133, 140, 148, 150-1, 155
Helford (Passage, River & Village) 16, 17, 18-26, 36, 38-9, 43, 47, 50, 61, 104, 151, 156, 159, *105*   See also FERRY BOAT INN.
Helston 76, 80-2, 101-3, 109, 119, 136, 145, 147-8, 150-1, 154, 157, 160, *110, 142*
Holidays 17, 20, 100, 117, 138, 142-3
Housel Bay Hotel 76
Housing 143-5, 147-8, *144, 145*

India 60, 99, 113-4, 123, *115*
Intelligence Operations 23, 25, 27-48, *24, 28, 32, 47, 48*
Isles of Scilly 25, 31, 34, 72, 87, 103

Landewednack 76
Lizard 59, 66-7, 69, 72, 75, 78, 82, 84, 87, 92, 102, 126-7, 129, 131, 143
Lomenech, Daniel 27-30, 33, 35, *28*
Looe 143
Lostwithiel 109, 119

Manaccan 146, 160, *118, 145, 149*
Marazion 127, 158
Mawnan Smith 22, 36, 88
Mevagissey 82
MGBs (Motor Gun Boats) 25, 34, 41-3, 45-7, 112, *38, 44*
Montgomery, Bernard Law 22, 135
Mullion 126-7, 143
Mutin 23, 38, 159, *24*

Nancekuke 87, 103, 131,133-4. See also PORTREATH.
Newquay 80, 117, 119, 119, 121, 143

Padstow 50, 56, 88
Par 82
Pendarves 157
Pen Olver 68, 74, 76, *74*
Penryn 52, 80, 88, 111-3, 146, 150
Perranporth 88, 90, 99, 117, 120
Perranwell 120
Penzance 62, 102, 120, 138, 154
Plymouth 21, 50, 66, 80, 113, 154, 156
Porthcurno 59-65, *61, 63, 64*
Porthleven 81, 138, 154, 157-8
Port Isaac 120
Portreath 70, 87-8, 90, 92-3, 95-7, 99-100, 102, 131, 134. See also
    NANCEKUKE.
Portscatho 138
Praa Sands 25, 47
Predannack 70, 87-8, 90, 92, 94-5, 97, 100-3, 126, 129, 130-1, *98, 101*
Probus 119

Radar 31, 54, 66-79, 80, 82, 84, 86, 90, 92-3, 95-6,˙123, *67, 71, 73, 75, 91*
See also DRY TREE, PEN OLVER, SENNEN, TRELANVEAN,
    TRELEAVER.
RAF See AIRFIELDS.
Rationing 50, 136, 138-9, 152, *139, 140*

Redruth 22, 92, 102, 111, 114, 120, 141, 147
"Rémy" 27, 29, 31-5, *30, 34, 37*
RNAS See CULDROSE, ST MERRYN.
ROC (Royal Observer Corps) 80-6, 110, *83, 85*
Roche 100
Ruan Major 127

St Agnes 82
St Anthony-in-Roseland 82
St Austell 119, 147
St Breward 80
St Columb Major 82, 119
St Day 108, 119
St Dennis 119
St Eval 38, 54, 66, 74, 87-8, 90, 97, 102, 131
St Ives 81, 143, 145, 154
St Just-in-Penwith 82, 97, 150
St Mawgan 97, 103, 113
St Merryn 54, 88, 96, 100, 103, *55,-7, 96, 99, 100*
Saltash 80
Schools 59, 129, 148, *149*
Sennen 72-4, 80-1
Swing Wing Project 128-131, *130. 132*

Trebah 17, 104, 156-7, *2, 17*
Tregony 109, 112
Tehidy 92, 150
Trelanvean 68-9
Treleaver 69-70, 75, 78, 84, 92, 95
Trelissick 9, 16, 104
Tolverne 9-17, 156, *9, 11*
Truro 10, 12, 50, 80-2, 84, 86, 97, 102, 107-12, 119-20, 124, 128, 138-40, 143-4,
    150-1, 153-4, 159
Turnaware 9-10, 12-3, 17, 156

US Servicemen 9-10, 13-4, 16, 36, 39, 40, 45, 54, 77, 84, 87, 97, 104, 106, 122,
144 ,157, *15, 105, 106*

VE and VJ Days 102, 109, 112, 119, 135, *108-10, 118-9*

Wallis, Barnes 123-4, 126, 128-31, *128*
Wrens (WRNS) 26, 49-58, 69, 96, 100, *4, 49, 51, 53, 55-8, 96, 99*

165

LANDFALL PUBLICATIONS

Also by Viv Acton & Derek Carter
OPERATION CORNWALL
See details overleaf.

Explore the places that feature in CORNISH WAR & PEACE
in the most enjoyable way - ON FOOT!
Bob Acton's
LANDFALL WALKS BOOKS
provide detailed directions plus lots of background information for round walks in the following areas:
The Fal, Helford and Fowey estuaries
The north coast of Cornwall from Padstow almost to Land's End
Most of the south coast from Penzance to Fowey
Many inland areas including those around Truro, Camborne, Redruth, Lostwithiel and St Austell

The books include sketch maps and are fully illustrated with sketches and photographs. Prices range from £1.25 to £4.95.

Kenneth Brown & Bob Acton
Exploring Cornish Mines £5.50
Guided tours of six important mine sites: Consols & United - Kitty & Blue Hills - Tywarnhayle - Basset - Dolcoath - Botallack to Boswedden.
Fully illustrated with photographs, diagrams and maps.
A second volume is planned for 1995.

OTHER LANDFALL BOOKS
St Ives Heritage (Lena & Donald Bray) £5.99
Newquay's Pictorial Past £3.00
Primrose Time (Mary Baker) (set in and around Lelant) £3.99
Launceston: Some Pages in History (Joan Rendell) £9.99
The Story of Port Navas (Peggy and Douglas Shepperd) £3.99

The books are available from local shops and direct from the publisher: see details at the front of this book.
Mail orders, please add 20% to cover postal costs, up to a maximum of £5.

OPERATION CORNWALL 1940-1944
The Fal, the Helford & D-Day
by Viv Acton & Derek Carter

Published to coincide with the 50th anniversary of D-Day, this fully illustrated book reveals the strategic importance - often overlooked in other studies - of this part of Cornwall.

Landfall Publications £5.99

Operation Cornwall is a book about the War years that will fascinate many people, from Falmouth to St Ives, with its mass of detail about everyday life during the War and with its overriding "feel" for the period. It is excellent value; a genuine celebration as much as a commemoration of remarkable times and of many ordinary but remarkable people.

St Ives Times & Echo

Little wonder that this evocative account .... is proving so popular. .... Highly recommended for all those who remember *and* those who are too young to do so.

Old Cornwall

.... such a well-written book .... The book is well illustrated, attractively produced and is a very good buy.

Cornwall Association of Local Historians Journal